Wonderful Curves
SAMPLER QUILT BLOCK BOOK

*This book of beautiful quilts is dedicated to
our dearest mother, Sherril Passey, who taught us
to be creative in all aspects of our lives.
Thank you for teaching by doing!*

Wonderful Curves Sampler Quilt Block Book

Landauer Publishing, www.landauerpub.com, is an imprint of Fox Chapel Publishing Company, Inc.

Project Team
Editor: Leslie T. Galliano
Copy Editor:
Designer: Wendy Reynolds
Photographer:
Indexer:

ISBN 978-1-947163-72-0

Library of Congress Control Number: 2021939888

We are always looking for talented authors. To submit an idea, please send a brief inquiry to
acquisitions@foxchapelpublishing.com.

Note to Professional Copy Services:
The publisher grants you permission to make up to six copies of any quilt patterns in this book for any customer
who purchased this book and states the copies are for personal use.

Printed in the United States of America
24 23 22 21 2 4 6 8 10 9 7 5 3 1

Wonderful Curves
SAMPLER QUILT BLOCK BOOK

30 Blocks • 14 Projects • Endless Possibilities

Jenny Pedigo,
Helen Robinson,
Sherilyn Mortensen

Landauer Publishing

Contents

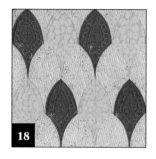
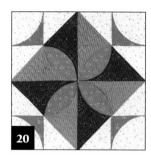

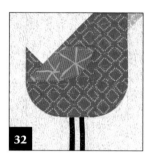

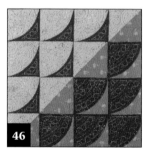
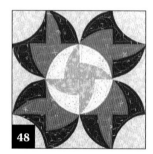

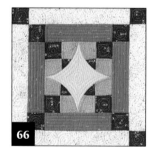
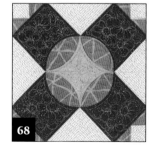
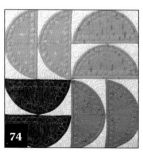
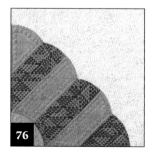

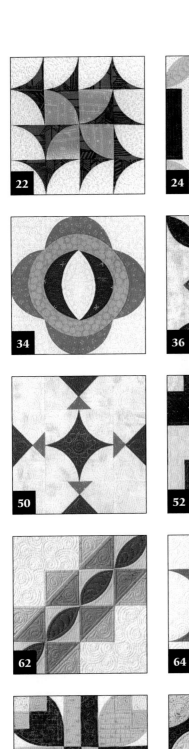
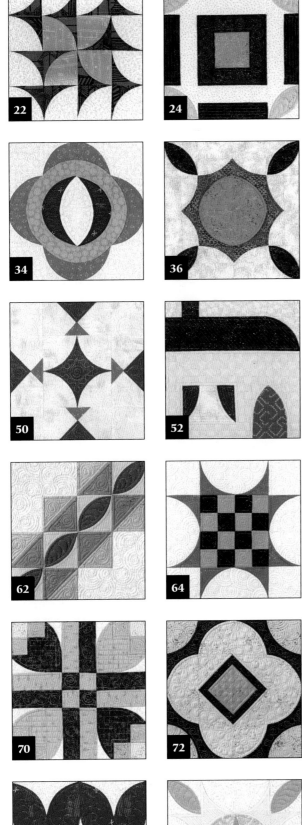
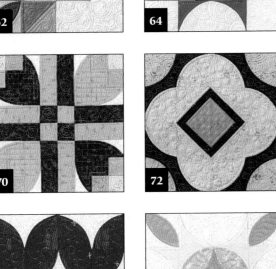

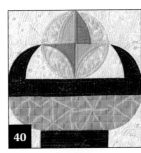
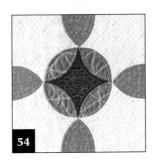

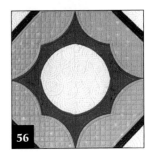

QUILT PATTERNS

Introduction

We are "sew" excited for our fourth book, *Wonderful Curves Sampler Quilt Block Book*! As with our other books, *Contemporary Curved Quilts, One Wonderful Curve,* and *Mini Wonderful Curves*, the focus is on easily cutting and sewing curves but with sampler blocks.

We love sampler quilts! They are so interesting to look at with each block having its own personality. We love the versatility of design and originality that come with color choices and layout options when working with 30 different blocks. We thought it would be fun to add curves to traditional blocks and to create some original blocks to mix in with traditional ones. We so enjoyed designing the 30 blocks in this book, which offer a fun mix of repeated elements, recognizeable objects, and medallion style blocks.

All designs in this book use our original notion, the Wonder Curve Ruler™. By using colored lines and markings on the Wonder Curve Ruler™, it is easier than ever to make complex curved piecing simply by matching up fabric to lines and then cutting, sewing, and squaring up.

—Helen, Sherilyn, and Jenny

Helen

Sherilyn

Jenny

You will need the Wonder Curve Ruler™ to complete the projects in this book.

Look for the Wonder Curve Ruler™ at your favorite quilt shop or visit Sewkindofwonderful.com for ordering information and ruler tutorials.

How to Use the Wonder Curve Ruler™

All projects in this book use the blue lines and marks on the Wonder Curve Ruler (WCR) to make cutting, sewing and squaring-up curved blocks fast and easy. We recommend making the following practice block to introduce you to cutting, sewing, and squaring up blocks as described throughout this book.

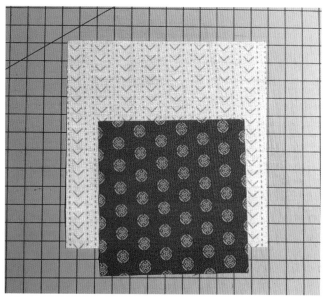

1. Cut (1) 4¼" x 4¼" and (1) 5¾" x 5¾"

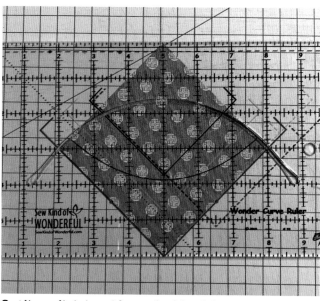

2. Align adjoining sides under blue 'V' on Wonder Curve Ruler (WCR). Cut in curve cut-out with rotary cutter.

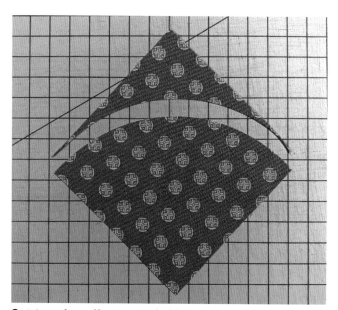

3. Discard small piece. Label large piece A.

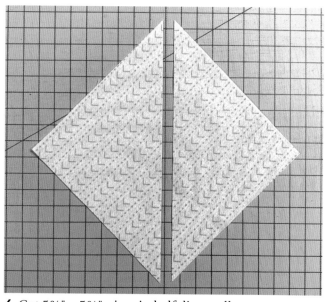

4. Cut 5¾" x 5¾" piece in half diagonally.

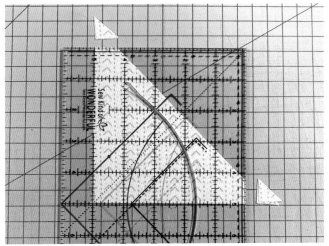

5. Stack both pieces and align 90° corner with 5" intersection and trim points extending beyond the ruler's edge.

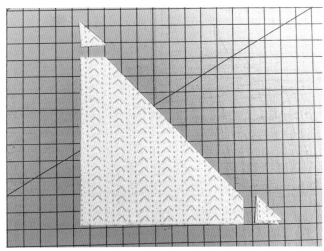

6. Discard small pieces.

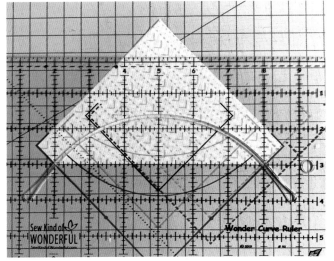

7. Align pieces under blue box corners on WCR as shown. Cut in curve cut-out with rotary cutter.

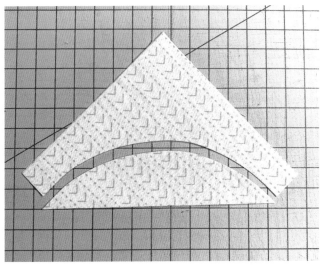

8. Discard small piece. Label large pieces B.

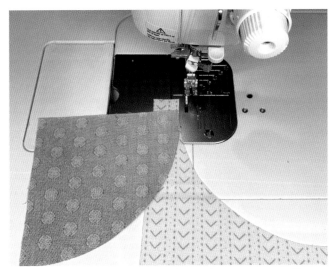

9. Lay out shapes A and B as shown leaving a ¼" tail.

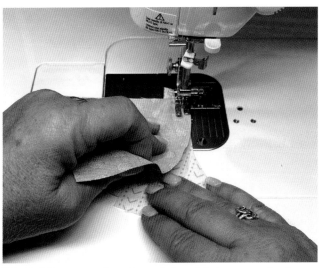

10. Holding one piece in each hand bring curved edges together as they feed under presser foot while stitching a ¼" seam. Refer to "How to Sew a Curve" on page 12.

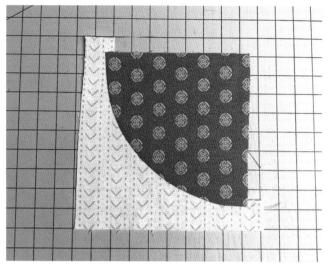

11. Press seam towards A. Label unit AB.

TIP: Never iron your curved blocks; instead, press with an up-and-down motion. Moving an iron back and forth over your blocks may distort them.

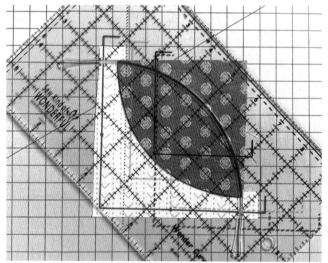

12. Position AB under WCR with curved seam aligned with blue curved line as shown. Cut in curve cut-out with rotary cutter.

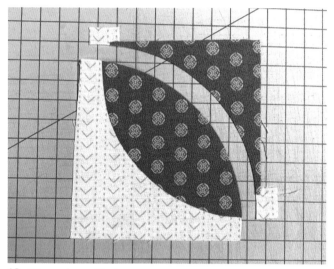

13. Discard small piece.

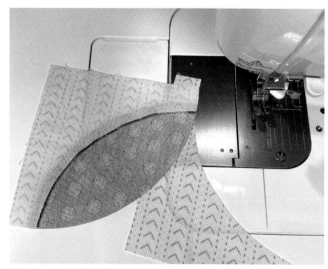

14. Lay out AB and B as shown leaving a ¼" tail.

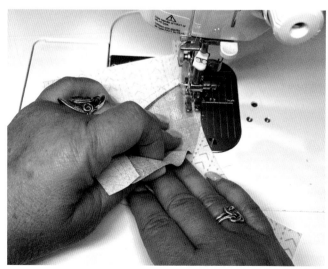

15. Sew curved seam.

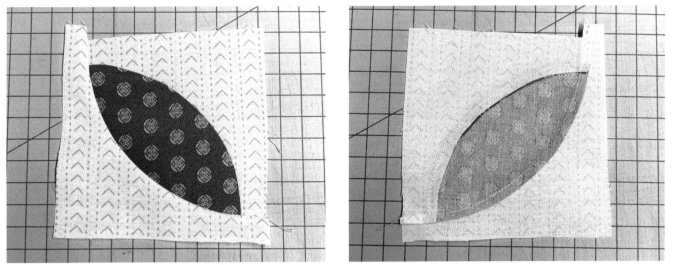

16. Press seam towards B. Label unit ABB or Citrus Block.

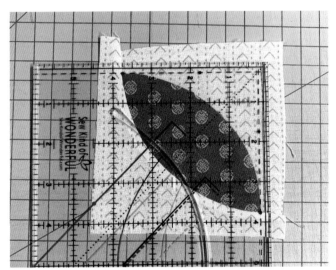

17. Square-up unit to 4" x 4". Position WCR on block with blue dots on points.

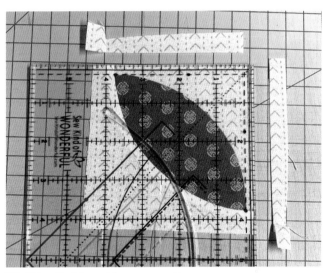

18. Trim 2 sides with rotary cutter.

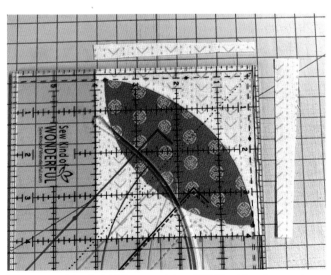

19. Rotate block 180°, reposition WCR with trimmed edges aligned with 4" marks. Trim remaining fabric.

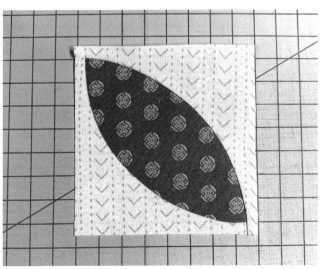

20. Citrus Block trimmed to 4" x 4.

How to Sew a Curve

Piecing the Curves

The curves will be pieced in the same manner in each project. Always use a ¼" seam allowance and sew with right sides together.

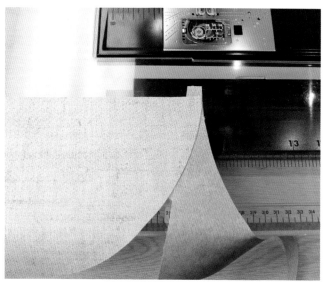

1. Position an A shape on a B shape, right sides together, with ¼" of B extending beyond A.

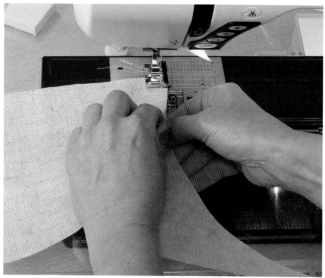

2. Hold one shape in each hand and slowly bring the curved edges together while stitching a ¼" seam.

TIP: When sewing the curves, always have the outside curve (the top piece) in your right hand and the inside curve (the bottom piece) in your left hand.

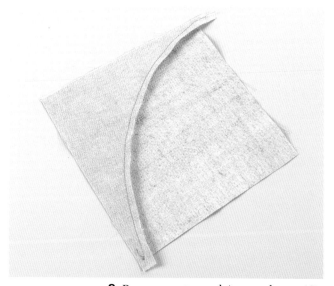

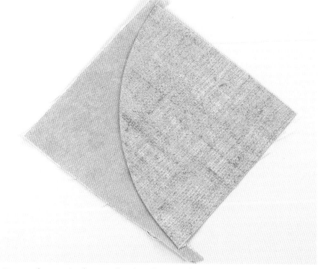

3. Press seam toward A to make an AB unit. Press the unit from the back and front.

How to Cut Specific Curves

We have given the different shapes cut with the WCR unique names to simplify the identification of various shapes and blocks throughout the patterns. The unique names come from the first Sew Kind of Wonderful pattern that used that particular shape.

Cutting Shimmer A & B

Position WCR on 5" x 5" square as shown with corner of fabric aligned with solid blue V. Cut in the curve cut-out with 45mm rotary cutter.

Note: One A and two B shapes make a Citrus Block. Individual patterns will explain how.

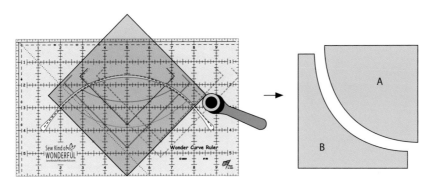

Cutting Shimmer A
Position WCR on 4¼" x 4¼" square as shown with corner of fabric aligned with solid blue V. Cut in the curve cut-out with 45mm rotary cutter.

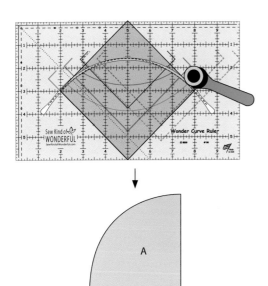

Cutting Shimmer B
Position WCR on 5¾" triangle with 90° corner aligned with 5" intersection as shown. Cut off points extending beyond WCR.

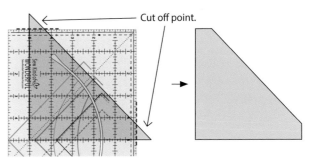

Cut off point.

Position fabric with corners aligned within blue box corners on WCR as shown. Cut in curve cut-out with rotary cutter to make B piece. Discard small piece.

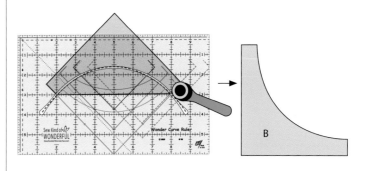

Cutting Twist C

Position WCR on 2¾" x 4½" rectangle with corner aligned at blue dashed corner as shown. Cut in the curve cut-out with rotary cutter to make C piece. Discard small piece.

Note: Fabric is positioned right side up (RSU) or right side down (RSD) according to pattern directions.

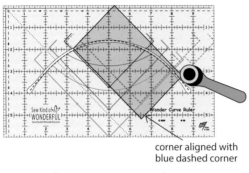

corner aligned with
blue dashed corner

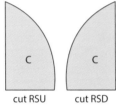

cut RSU   cut RSD

Cutting Twist D

Position WCR on 3½" x 5" rectangle with corner aligned at the blue dashed corner as shown. Cut in the curve cut-out with rotary cutter to make C and D pieces.

Note: Not all patterns use C. Discard if indicated in pattern. It is not possible to cut D without cutting C also.

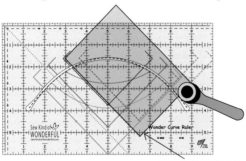

corner aligned with
blue dashed corner

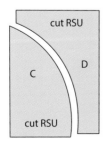 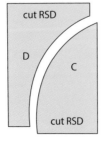

Cutting Antler F & Twist C

Position WCR on 5" x 5" with corner aligned at the blue dashed corner as shown. Cut in the curve cut-out with rotary cutter to make F and C pieces.

Note: Not all patterns use C. Discard if indicated in pattern. It is not possible to cut F without cutting a C also.

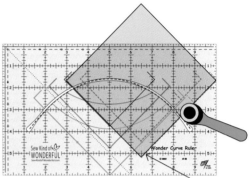

corner aligned with
blue dashed corner

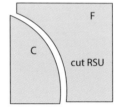 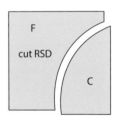

Wonder Curve Ruler™

This 6" x 10" piecing ruler has colored lines and markings making it wonderfully simple to use for the combination of curved blocks, which are used repeatedly in the patterns featured in this book.

These unique lines and markings make using the Wonder Curve Ruler easy as, 1-2-3. The three bold, colored lines also make it easy to scale a block larger or smaller just by aligning fabric with the different colors and marks.

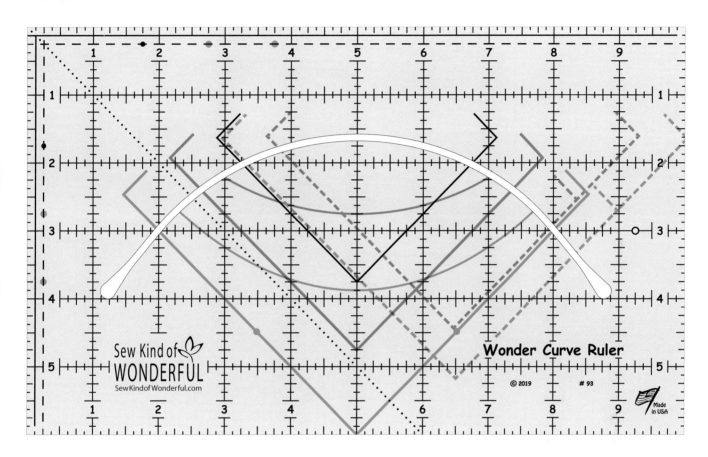

Video Tutorial

For a video on using the Wonder Curve Ruler™ head on over to the Sew Kind of Wonderful You Tube Channel www.youtube.com/watch?v=gOpt5UhjAGQ&t=3s.

Sampler Blocks

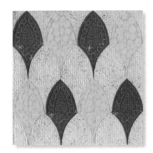

Block 1 - Shell Chain

Unfinished block size: 14½" x 14½"

MATERIALS FOR 1 BLOCK
✛ 1 each fat eighth focus fabric in green and citrine
✛ 1 fat quarter background fabric in peach
✛ Wonder Curve Ruler™ (WCR)

GENERAL CUTTING
From each focus fabric, cut:
✛ (8) 3½" x 5" rectangles
From background fabric, cut:
✛ (16) 3½" x 5" rectangles

Cut the Curves

Refer to page 14 to cut the following Twist shapes with WCR.

Green and citrine focus fabrics:
Twist C & D
From (16) 3½" x 5" rectangles, cut eight C and eight D curves, four right side up (RSU) and four right side down (RSD), in each color.

4 each cut RSU   4 each cut RSD

Background fabric:
Twist C & D
From (16) 3½" x 5" rectangles, cut sixteen C and sixteen D curves, eight RSU and eight RSD.

8 each cut RSU   8 each cut RSD

Sew the Curves

1. Lay out the following sets:

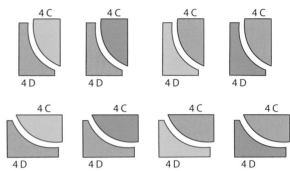

2. Position C on D, right sides together, with ¼" of D extending beyond C as shown. Holding one piece in each hand, bring curved edges together as they feed under the presser foot while stitching a ¼" seam (see page 12). Repeat to sew all CD sets. Press seam towards C.

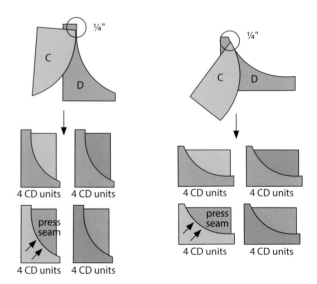

Square Up the Units

3. Square up the CD blocks to 2¼" x 4". Position WCR on blocks as shown with the blue dot on curved seam and 2" mark on curved seam. Trim side and top. Rotate block and align trimmed edges with 2¼" and 4" marks. Trim remaining fabric.

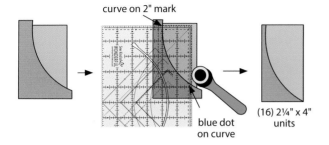

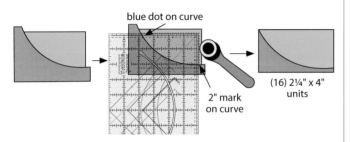

Custom Quilting Detail

Assemble the Block

4. Lay out CD units as shown. Sew to form rows. Press seams open. Sew rows together. Press seams open.

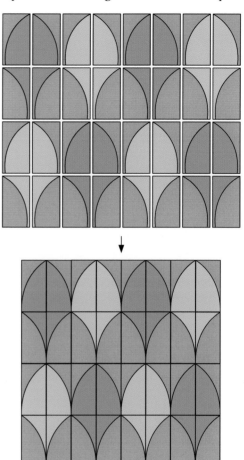

Block Assembly Diagram

Alternate Color & Layout Options

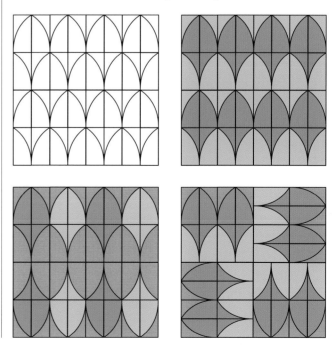

Block 2 - Petal Pusher

Unfinished block size: 14½" x 14½"

MATERIALS FOR 1 BLOCK
✢ 1 each fat eighth focus fabric in green, pink, and mauve
✢ (1) 10" x 20" neutral background fabric
✢ Wonder Curve Ruler™ (WCR)

GENERAL CUTTING
From green focus fabric, cut:
✢ (4) 5" x 5" squares
From each pink and mauve focus fabric, cut:
✢ (2) 5" x 5" squares
✢ (2) 5¾" x 5¾" squares
From background fabric, cut:
✢ (4) 5" x 5" squares
✢ (4) 4¼" x 4¼" squares

Cut the Curves
Refer to page 13 to cut the following Shimmer shapes with WCR.

Green focus fabric:
Shimmer A & B
From four 5" x 5" squares, cut two A curves and two B curves.

Pink focus fabric:
Shimmer B
From two 5¾" x 5¾" squares cut in half diagonally, cut four B curves.

Mauve focus fabric:
Shimmer B
From two 5¾" x 5¾" squares cut in half diagonally, cut four B curves.

Background fabric:
Shimmer A
From four 4¼" x 4¼" squares, cut four A curves.

Sew the Curves
1. Lay out the following sets:

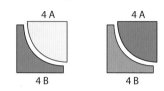

2. Position A on B, right sides together (RST), with ¼" of B extending beyond A as shown. Holding one piece in each hand, bring curved edges together as they feed under the presser foot while stitching a ¼" seam (see page 12). Repeat to sew all AB sets. Press seam towards A.

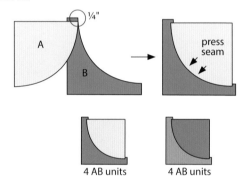

3. Working with four AB green/pink units only, position AB under WCR with curved seam aligned with the blue curved line as shown. Cut in the curve cut-out. Discard small piece.

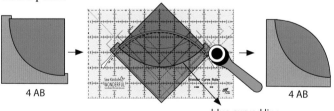

4. Lay out AB trimmed units and four B mauve pieces as shown. Position AB on B, RST, with a ¼" tail of B extending beyond AB. Sew curved seam to make ABB unit. Press seam towards B. Repeat for remaining set.

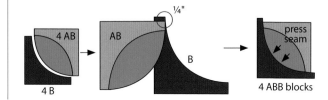

Square Up the Units

5. Square up AB and ABB blocks to 4" x 4". Position WCR on blocks as shown with the blue dots on curved seams and points. Trim side and top. Rotate block and align trimmed edges with 4" marks and trim remaining fabric. Repeat for all AB and ABB blocks.

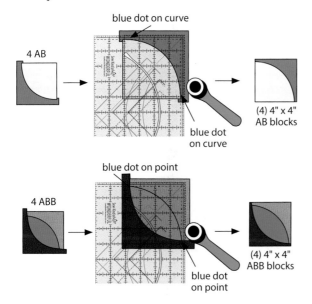

Make Half-Square Triangles

6. Make eight half-square triangle (HST) blocks. Draw a line diagonally on wrong side of four 5" x 5" background squares. Layer, RST, with two 5" x 5" pink and two 5" x 5" mauve squares. Sew ¼" from drawn line on each side. Cut in half on drawn line. Press open. Square up all eight HSTs to 4" x 4" squares.

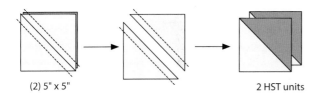

Make 8 HSTs.

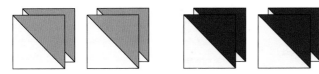

Square up all 8 HSTs to 4" x 4".

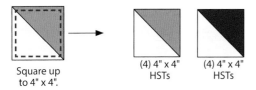

Assemble the Block

7. Lay out units as shown. Sew to form rows. Press seams open. Sew rows together. Press seams open.

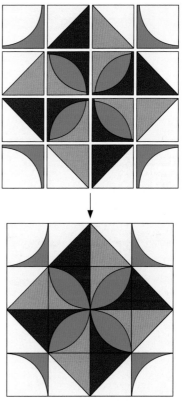

Block Assembly Diagram

Alternate Color & Layout Options

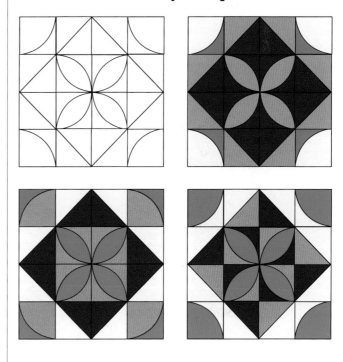

Block 3 - Goose Tag

Unfinished block size: 14½" x 14½"

MATERIALS FOR 1 BLOCK
✛ 1 fat quarter geese fabric in green
✛ (1) 10" x 10" center pinwheel fabric in gold
✛ One fat quarter neutral background fabric
✛ Wonder Curve Ruler™ (WCR)

GENERAL CUTTING
From green geese fabric, cut:
✛ (8) 5¾" x 5¾" squares
From gold pinwheel fabric, cut:
✛ (4) 4¼" x 4¼" squares
From background fabric, cut:
✛ (12) 4¼" x 4¼" squares

Cut the Curves
Refer to page 13 to cut the following Shimmer shapes with the WCR.

Green geese fabric:
Shimmer B
From eight 5¾" x 5¾" squares cut in half diagonally, cut sixteen B curves.

16 B

Gold pinwheel fabric:
Shimmer A
From four 4¼" x 4¼" squares, cut four A curves.

4 A

Background fabric:
Shimmer A
From twelve 4¼" x 4¼" squares, cut twelve A curves.

12 A

Sew the Curves
1. Lay out the following sets:

12 A / 12 B

4 A / 4 B

2. Position A on B, right sides together, with ¼" of B extending beyond A as shown. Holding one piece in each hand, bring curved edges together as they feed under the presser foot while stitching a ¼" seam (see page 12). Repeat to sew all AB sets. Press seam towards B.

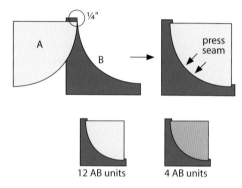

12 AB units   4 AB units

Square Up the Units
3. Square up AB to 4" x 4". Position WCR on blocks as shown with blue dots on curved seams. Trim side and top. Rotate block and align trimmed edges with 4" marks and trim remaining fabric. Repeat for all AB blocks.

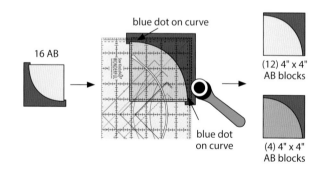

16 AB   blue dot on curve   (12) 4" x 4" AB blocks

blue dot on curve   (4) 4" x 4" AB blocks

Assemble the Block

4. Lay out units as shown. Sew to form rows. Press seams open. Sew rows together. Press seams open.

Block Assembly Diagram

Alternate Color & Layout Options

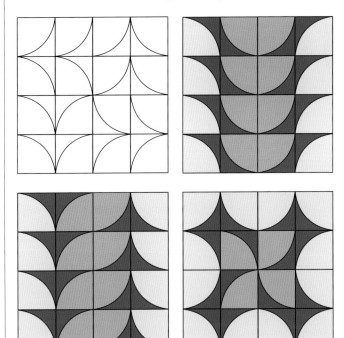

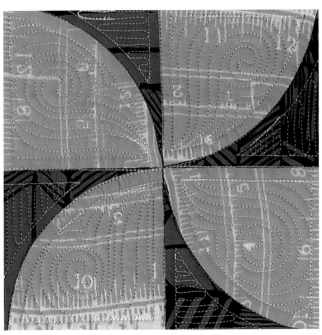

Custom Quilting Detail

Block 4 - Stained Glass

Unfinished block size: 14½" x 14½"

MATERIALS FOR 1 BLOCK
✛ (1) 5" x 5" accent fabric in blue
✛ 1 each 10" x 10" focus fabric in maroon, black, and pink
✛ 1 fat quarter neutral background fabric
✛ Wonder Curve Ruler™ (WCR)

GENERAL CUTTING
From blue accent fabric, cut:
✛ (1) 4" x 4" squares
From maroon focus fabric, cut:
✛ (2) 2¼" x 7½" rectangles
✛ (2) 2¼" x 4" rectangles
From black focus fabric, cut:
✛ (4) 2¼" x 7½" rectangles
From pink focus fabric, cut:
✛ (4) 4¼" x 4¼" squares
From background fabric, cut:
✛ (4) 2¼" x 7½" rectangles
✛ (4) 5¾" x 5¾" squares

Cut the Curves

Refer to page 13 to cut the following Shimmer shapes with the WCR.

Pink focus fabric:
Shimmer A
From four 4¼" x 4¼" squares, cut four A curves.

Background fabric:
Shimmer B
From four 5¾" x 5¾" squares cut in half diagonally, cut eight B curves.

Sew the Curves

1. Lay out the following sets:

2. Position A on B, right sides together (RST), with ¼" of B extending beyond A as shown. Holding one piece in each hand, bring curved edges together as they feed under the presser foot while stitching a ¼" seam (see page 12). Repeat to sew all AB sets. Press seam towards A.

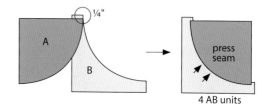

3. Working with four AB blue/pink units only, position AB under WCR with curved seam aligned with the blue curved line as shown. Cut in the curve cut-out. Discard small piece.

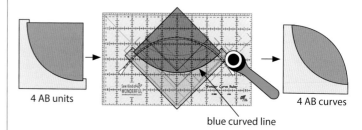

blue curved line

4. Lay out the trimmed AB units and four background B curves as shown. Position AB on B, RST, with a ¼" tail of B extending beyond AB as shown. Sew curved seam to make ABB units. Press seam towards B. Repeat for remaining sets.

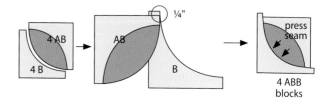

Square Up the Units

5. Square up ABB units to 4" x 4". Position WCR on blocks with blue dots on points as shown. Trim side and top. Rotate block and align trimmed edges with 4" marks and trim remaining fabric. Repeat for all ABB blocks.

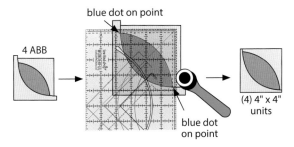

Make the Center Unit

6. Lay out the rectangles around the center squares as shown. Sew left and right pieces to the center, then press seams. Sew the top and bottom pieces to the unit, then press seams.

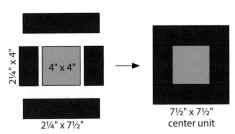

Custom Quilting Detail

Assemble the Block

7. Lay out units as shown. Sew boxed sections together first. Press seams. Sew to form rows, then press seams open. Sew rows together, and then press seams open.

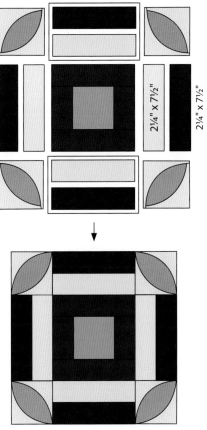

Block Assembly Diagram

Alternate Color & Layout Options

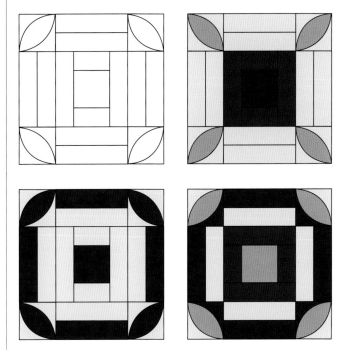

Block 5 - Treasure Box

Unfinished block size: 14½" x 14½"

MATERIALS FOR 1 BLOCK
- ✛ (1) 10" x 10" focus fabric in light pink
- ✛ (1) 12" x 12" focus fabric in dark orange
- ✛ 1 fat quarter focus fabric in light orange
- ✛ (1) 6" x 12" focus fabric in blue
- ✛ (1) 10" x 10" neutral background fabric
- ✛ Wonder Curve Ruler™ (WCR)

GENERAL CUTTING
From light pink focus fabric, cut:
- ✛ (4) 4¼" x 4¼" squares

From dark orange focus fabric, cut:
- ✛ (4) 5¾" x 5¾" squares

From light orange focus fabric, cut:
- ✛ (4) 5" x 5" squares
- ✛ (2) 5¾" x 5¾" squares

From blue focus fabric, cut:
- ✛ (2) 5½" x 5½ squares

From background fabric, cut:
- ✛ (2) 5½" x 5½ squares
- ✛ (4) 4¼" x 4¼" squares

Cut the Curves

Refer to page 13 to cut the following Shimmer shapes with the WCR.

Light pink focus fabric:
Shimmer A
From four 4¼" x 4¼" squares, cut four A curves.

4 A

Dark orange focus fabric:
Shimmer B
From four 5¾" x 5¾" squares cut in half diagonally, cut eight B curves.

8 B

Light orange focus fabric:
Shimmer B
From two 5¾" x 5¾" squares cut in half diagonally, cut four B curves

4 B

Background fabric:
Shimmer A
From four 4¼" x 4¼" squares, cut four A curves.

4 A

Sew the Curves

1. Lay out the following sets:

4 A / 4 B   4 A / 4 B

2. Position A on B, right sides together (RST), with ¼" of B extending beyond A as shown. Holding one piece in each hand, bring curved edges together as they feed under the presser foot while stitching a ¼" seam (see page 12). Repeat to sew all AB sets. Press seam towards A.

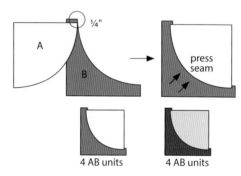

¼"

A

B

press seam

4 AB units   4 AB units

3. Working with four AB dark orange/light pink units only, position AB under WCR with curved seam aligned with the blue curved line as shown. Cut in the curve cut-out. Discard small piece.

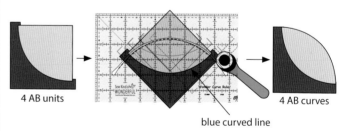

4 AB units   4 AB curves

blue curved line

4. Lay out the trimmed AB curves and four dark orange B curves as shown. Position AB on B, RST, with a ¼" tail of B extending beyond AB as shown. Sew curved seam to make ABB block. Press seam towards B. Repeat for remaining sets.

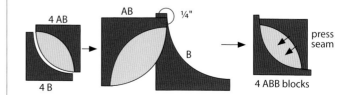

4 AB   AB   ¼"

press seam

4 B   B   4 ABB blocks

Square Up the Units

5. Square up the AB and ABB blocks to 4" x 4". Position WCR on blocks as shown with blue dots on curved seams or points. Trim side and top. Rotate block and align trimmed edges with 4" marks and trim remaining fabric. Repeat for all AB and ABB blocks.

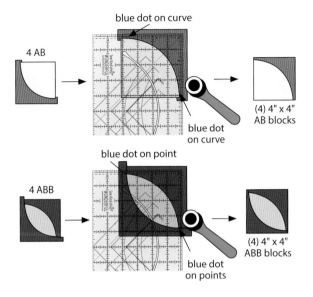

Make Half-Quarter Triangle Units

6. Make eight half-quarter triangle (HQT) blocks. Draw a line diagonally on wrong side of 5½" x 5½" background square. Layer, RST, with 5½" x 5½" blue square. Sew ¼" from drawn line on each side. Cut in half on drawn line. Press open. Draw a diagonal line on wrong side of one half-square triangle block. Layer with light orange 5" background square, RST. Sew ¼" from drawn line on each side. Cut on drawn line. Press open. Trim both to 4" x 4".

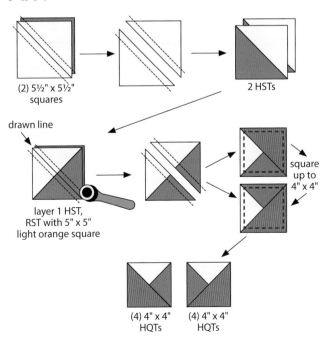

Assemble the Block

7. Lay out units as shown. Sew to form rows. Press seams open. Sew rows together, then press seams open.

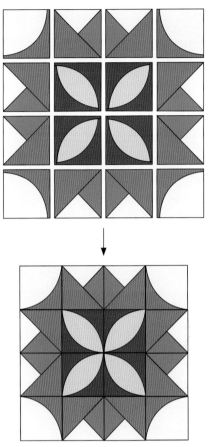

Block Assembly Diagram

Alternate Color & Layout Options

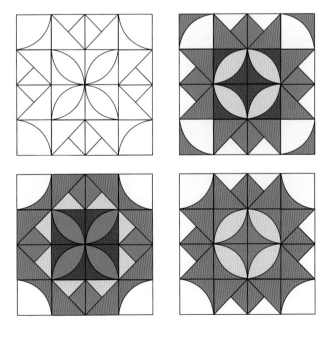

Block 6 - Lotus Blossom

Unfinished block size: 14½" x 14½"

MATERIALS FOR 1 BLOCK
+ 1 each fat eighth fabric in coral and brown
+ 1 each 10" x 10" focus fabrics in orange and dark orange
+ 1 fat quarter neutral background fabric
+ Wonder Curve Ruler™ (WCR)

GENERAL CUTTING
From each coral and brown focus fabric, cut:
+ (2) 4¼" x 4¼" squares
+ (8) 2¾" x 4½" rectangles
From each orange and dark orange focus fabric, cut:
+ (1) 5¾" x 5¾" square
+ (4) 2¼" x 2¼" squares
From background fabric, cut
+ (16) 3½" x 5" rectangles
+ (8) 2¼" x 2¼" squares

Cut the Curves

Refer to pages 13 and 14 to cut the following Shimmer and Twist shapes with WCR.

Coral and brown focus fabrics:
Shimmer A

From four 4¼" x 4¼" squares, cut two coral A curves and two mauve A curves.

Twist C

From (16) 2¾" x 4½" rectangles, cut four C coral curves right side up (RSU); four C mauve coral curves RSU; four C coral curves right side down (RSD); and four C mauve curves RSD.

Orange and dark orange focus fabrics:
Shimmer B

From both 5¾" x 5¾" squares cut in half diagonally, cut two orange curves and two dark orange curves.

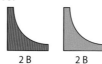

Background fabric:
Twist D

From (16) 3½" x 5" rectangles, cut eight D curves RSU and eight D curves RSD.

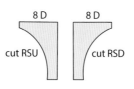

Sew the Curves

1. Lay out the following sets:

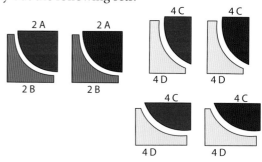

2. Position A on B, right side together (RST), with ¼" of B extending beyond A as shown. Holding one piece in each hand, bring curved edges together as they feed under the presser foot while stitching a ¼" seam (see page 12). Repeat to sew all AB sets. Press seam towards A.

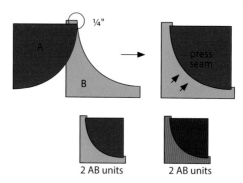

3. Position C on D, RST, with ¼" of D extending beyond C. Holding one piece in each hand, bring curved edges together as they feed under the presser foot while stitching a ¼" seam. Repeat to sew all CD sets. Press seam towards C.

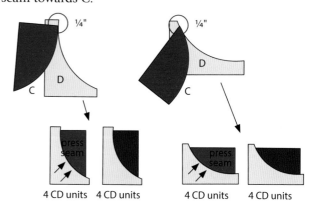

Square Up the Units

4. Square up the AB units to 4" x 4". Position WCR on blocks as shown with the blue dots on curved seams. Trim side and top. Rotate block and align trimmed edges with 4" marks and trim remaining fabric. Repeat for all AB blocks.

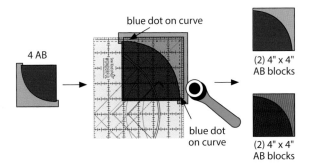

5. Square up the CD units to 2¼" x 4". Position WCR on block as shown with blue dot on curved seam and 2" mark on curved seam. Trim side and top. Rotate block and align trimmed edges with 2¼" and 4" marks and trim remaining fabric.

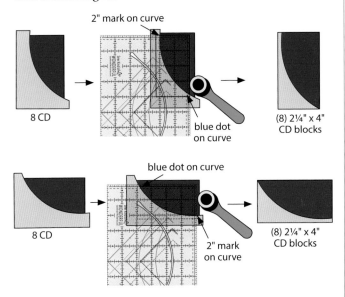

Make Corner Units

6. Lay out one 2¼" x 2¼" orange square, one 2¼" x 2¼" dark orange square, and two 2¼" x 2¼" background squares as shown. Sew to form rows. Press seams. Sew rows together, then press seam. Repeat to make four 4-patch blocks.

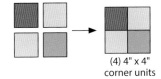

Assemble the Block

7. Lay out units as shown. Sew boxed sections together first. Press seams open. Sew to form rows, then press seams open. Sew rows together. Press seams open.

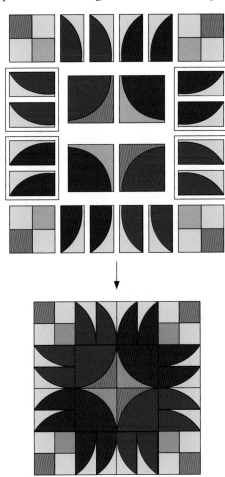

Block Assembly Diagram

Alternate Color & Layout Options

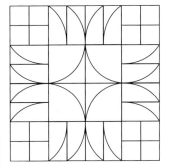

Block 7 - Beech Tree

Unfinished block size: 14½" x 14½"

MATERIALS FOR 1 BLOCK
✛ 1 each fat eighth for leaves in yellow and green
✛ (1) 5" x 5" accent fabric for leaves in red
✛ (1) 10" x 10" tree trunk fabric in brown
✛ (1) 12" x 12" neutral background fabric
✛ Wonder Curve Ruler™ (WCR)

GENERAL CUTTING
From each yellow and green leaves fabric, cut:
✛ (17) 2¼" x 2¼" yellow squares
✛ (18) 2¼" x 2¼" green squares
✛ (3) 2¼" x 2¼" red squares
From tree trunk fabric, cut:
✛ (2) 4" x 4" squares
✛ (1) 5¾" x 5¾" square
From background fabric, cut:
✛ (2) 4¼" x 4¼" squares
✛ (4) 2¼" x 4" rectangles
✛ (2) 2¼" x 2¼" squares

Cut the Curves
Refer to page 13 to cut the following Shimmer shapes with the WCR.

Tree trunk fabric:
Shimmer B
From the 5¾" x 5¾" square cut in half diagonally, cut two B curves.

2 B

Background fabric:
Shimmer A
From two 4¼" x 4¼" squares, cut two A curves.

2 A

Sew the Curves
1. Lay out the following sets:

2 A

2 B

2. Position A on B, right sides together, with ¼" of B extending beyond A as shown. Holding one piece in each hand, bring curved edges together as they feed under the presser foot while stitching a ¼" seam (see page 12). Repeat to sew all AB sets. Press seam towards B.

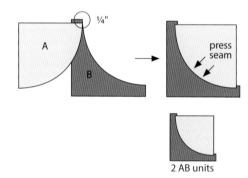

2 AB units

Square Up the Units
3. Square up AB blocks to 4" x 4". Position WCR on blocks as shown with the blue dots on curved seams. Trim side and top. Rotate block and align trimmed edges with 4" marks and trim remaining fabric. Repeat for all AB blocks.

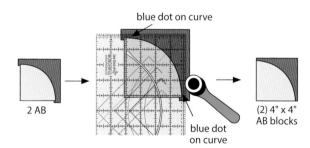

blue dot on curve

2 AB

blue dot on curve

(2) 4" x 4" AB blocks

Assemble the Block

4. Lay out units as shown. Sew boxed sections together first and press seams. Sew to form rows. Press seams. Sew rows together, then press seams.

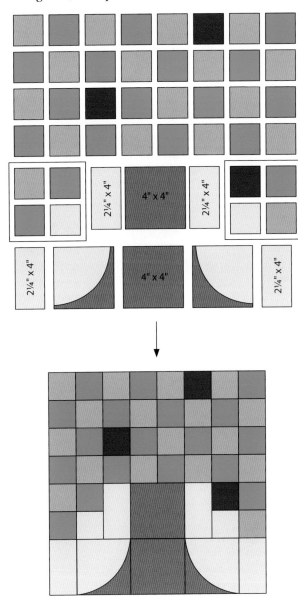

Block Assembly Diagram

Alternate Color Options

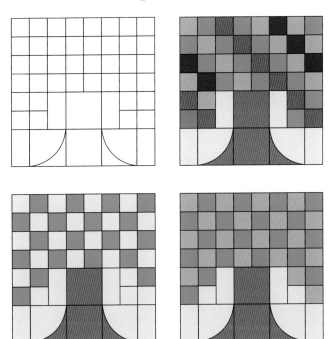

Custom Quilting Detail

Block 8 - Birdie

Unfinished block size: 14½" x 14½"

MATERIALS FOR 1 BLOCK
✤ 1 fat quarter bird fabric in blue
✤ (1) 5" x 10" wing fabric in orange
✤ (1) 2¼" x 2¼" beak fabric in yellow
✤ (1) 2" x 4" leg fabric in black
✤ 1 fat quarter neutral background fabric
✤ Wonder Curve Ruler™ (WCR)

GENERAL CUTTING

From blue bird fabric, cut:
✤ (1) 5½" x 5½" square
✤ (2) 5" x 5" squares
✤ (3) 4" x 4" squares

From orange wing fabric, cut:
✤ (1) 5" x 5" square
✤ (1) 4¼" x 4¼" square

From beak fabric, cut:
✤ (1) 2¼" x 2¼" square

From black leg fabric, cut:
✤ (2) 1" x 4" rectangles

From background fabric, cut:
✤ (1) 5¾" x 5¾" square
✤ (1) 5½" x 5½" square
✤ (3) 4" x 4" squares
✤ (2) 2¼" x 14½" rectangles
✤ (2) 1½" x 4" rectangles
✤ (1) 1" x 4" rectangle

Cut the Curves

Refer to page 13 cut the following Shimmer shapes with the WCR.

Blue bird fabric:
Shimmer A & B
From two 5" x 5" squares, cut two A curves and one B curve.

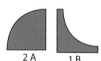

Orange wing fabric:
Shimmer A
From the 4¼" x 4¼" square, cut one A curve.

Background fabric:
Shimmer B
From the 5¾" x 5¾" square cut in half diagonally, cut two B curves.

Sew the Curves

1. Lay out the following sets:

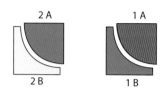

2. Position A on B, right sides together (RST), with ¼" of B extending beyond A as shown. Holding one piece in each hand, bring curved edges together as they feed under the presser foot while stitching a ¼" seam (see page 12). Repeat to sew all AB sets. Press seam towards B.

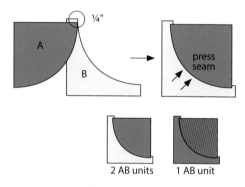

Square Up the Units

3. Square up the AB units to 4" x 4". Position WCR on blocks as shown with the blue dots on curved seams. Trim side and top. Rotate block and align trimmed edges with 4" marks and trim remaining fabric. Repeat for all AB blocks.

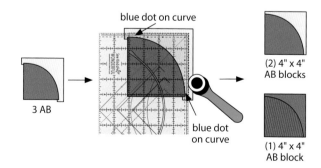

Make the Bird Unit

4. Make one half-square triangle (HST) and one half-quarter triangle (HQT). Draw a line diagonally on wrong side of 5½" x 5½" background square. Layer, RST, with 5½" x 5½" bird square. Sew ¼" from drawn line on each side. Cut in half on drawn line. Press open. Square up one to 4" x 4". On other HST, draw a diagonal line on wrong side. Layer with 5" orange wing square, RST, to make the HQT unit. Sew ¼" from drawn line on each side. Cut on drawn line. Press open. Trim both to 4" x 4". Select appropriate HQT for a right or left facing bird. Discard remaining HQT.

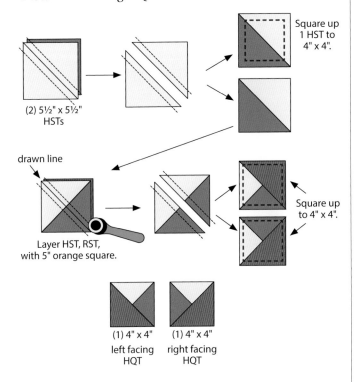

(2) 5½" x 5½" HSTs

Square up 1 HST to 4" x 4".

drawn line

Layer HST, RST, with 5" orange square.

Square up to 4" x 4".

(1) 4" x 4" left facing HQT

(1) 4" x 4" right facing HQT

5. Lay out the black bird leg and neutral background pieces as shown. Sew together. Press seams towards bird legs.

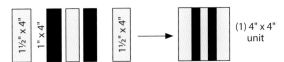

1½" x 4"   1" x 4"   1½" x 4"

(1) 4" x 4" unit

6. Draw a diagonal line on wrong side of the 2¼" beak square. Position on 2¼" x 14½" background piece as shown. Sew on drawn line. Trim ¼" from seam. Press open.

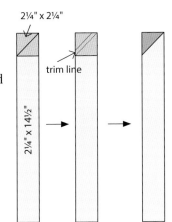

2¼" x 2¼"

trim line

2¼" x 14½"

Assemble the Block

7. Lay out units as shown. Sew to form rows. Press seams. Sew rows together, then press seams. Sew side sections to bird body. Press seams.

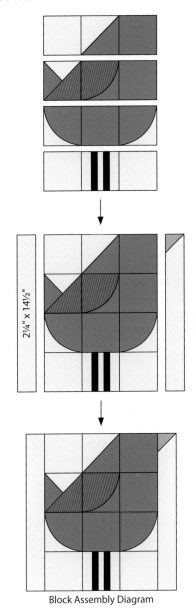

2¼" x 14½"

Block Assembly Diagram

Alternate Color & Layout Options

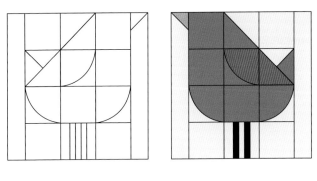

Block 9 - Locket

Unfinished block size: 14½" x 14½"

MATERIALS FOR 1 BLOCK
✛ (1) 10" x 20" focus fabric in teal
✛ (1) 12" x 20" focus fabric in green
✛ (1) 10" x 10" focus fabric in fuchsia
✛ 1 fat quarter neutral background fabric
✛ Wonder Curve Ruler™ (WCR)

GENERAL CUTTING
From teal focus fabric, cut:
✛ (8) 5" x 5" squares
From green focus fabric, cut:
✛ (2) 5¾" x 5¾" squares
✛ (8) 2¾" x 4½" rectangles
From fuchsia focus fabric, cut:
✛ (4) 5" x 5" squares
From background fabric, cut:
✛ (4) 5¾" x 5¾" squares
✛ (4) 2¾" x 4½" rectangles
✛ (4) 4" x 4" squares

Cut the Curves

Refer to pages 13 and 14 to cut the following Antler, Shimmer, and Twist shapes with the WCR.

Teal focus fabric:
Antler F
From eight 5" x 5" squares right sides together (RST), cut four F curves right side up (RSU) and four F curves right side down (RSD).

Green focus fabric:
Shimmer B
From two 5¾" x 5¾" squares cut in half diagonally, cut four B curves.

Twist C
From eight 2¾" x 4½" rectangles, cut four C curves RSU and four C curves RSD.

Fuchsia focus fabric:
Antler F
From four 5" x 5" squares, cut, RST, two F curves RSU and two F curves RSD.

Background fabric:
Shimmer B
From four 5¾" x 5¾" squares cut in half diagonally, cut eight B curves.

Twist C
From four 2¾" x 4½" rectangles, cut, RST, two C curves RSU and two C curves RSD.

Sew the Curves

1. Lay out the following sets:

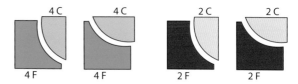

2. Position C on F, RST, as shown, matching ends or leaving a ¾" tail as indicated. Sew curved seam (see page 12). Press seam towards F.

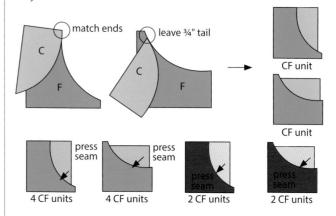

3. Position WCR on CF as shown with circle on V line on curved seam. Cut in curve cut-out. Discard small pieces. Repeat for all CF units.

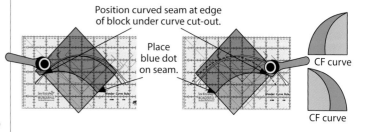

4. Position CF on B, RST, as shown, leaving a ¼" tail. Sew the curved seam to make CFB. Press seam towards B.

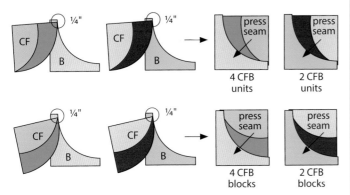

Square Up the Units

5. Square up the CFB blocks to 4" x 4". Position WCR on blocks as shown with the blue dots on curved seam or point. Trim side and top. Rotate block and align trimmed edges with 4" marks and trim remaining fabric. Repeat for all CFB blocks.

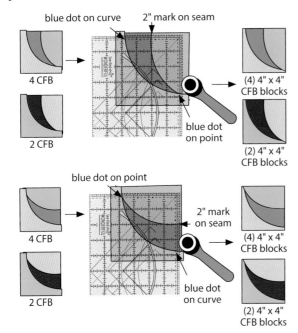

Assemble the Block

6. Lay out units as shown. Sew to form rows, then press seams open. Sew rows together. Press seams open.

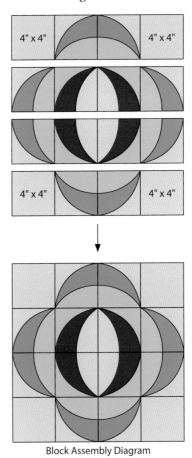

Block Assembly Diagram

Alternate Color & Layout Options

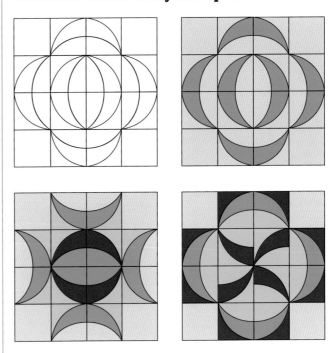

Block 10 - Sunburst

Unfinished block size: 14½" x 14½"

MATERIALS FOR 1 BLOCK
✤ (1) 10" x 10" focus fabric in eggplant and orange
✤ 1 fat quarter focus fabric in coral
✤ 1 fat quarter neutral background fabric
✤ Wonder Curve Ruler™ (WCR)

GENERAL CUTTING
From each of the orange and eggplant focus fabric, cut:
✤ (4) 4¼" x 4¼" squares
From coral focus, cut:
✤ (2) 5¾" x 5¾" squares
✤ (8) 3½" x 5" rectangles
From background fabric, cut:
✤ (4) 5¾" x 5¾" squares
✤ (4) 2¼" x 7½" rectangles
✤ (8) 2¾" x 4½" rectangles

Cut the Curves

Refer to pages 13 and 14 to cut the following Shimmer and Twist shapes using the WCR.

Orange focus fabric:
Shimmer A
From four 4¼" x 4¼" squares, cut four A curves.

Eggplant focus fabric:
Shimmer A
From four 4¼" x 4¼" squares, cut four A curves.

Coral focus fabric:
Shimmer B
From two 5¾" x 5¾" squares cut in half diagonally, cut four B curves.

Twist D
From eight 3½" x 5" rectangles, cut four D curves right side up (RSU) and four D curves right side down (RSD).

Background fabric:
Shimmer B
From four 5¾" x 5¾" squares cut in half diagonally, cut eight B curves.

Twist C
From eight 2¾" x 4½" rectangles, cut four C curves RSU and four C curves RSD.

Sew the Curves

1. Lay out the following sets:

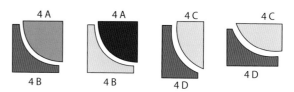

2. Position A on B, right sides together (RST), with ¼" of B extending beyond A as shown. Holding one piece in each hand, bring curved edges together as they feed under the presser foot while stitching a ¼" seam (see page 12). Repeat to sew all AB sets. Press seam towards A.

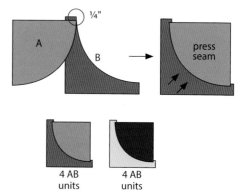

3. Working with four AB eggplant and background units only, position AB under WCR with curved seam aligned with the blue curved line as shown. Cut in the curve cut-out. Discard small piece.

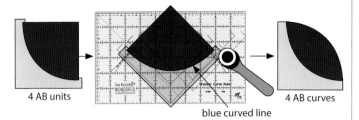

4. Lay out AB trimmed units and four B background pieces. Position AB on B, RST, with a ¼" tail of B extending beyond AB as shown. Sew curved seam to make ABB units. Press seam towards B. Repeat for remaining set.

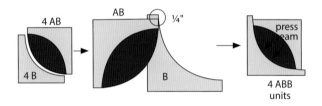

5. Position C on D, RST, with ¼" of D extending beyond C. Holding one piece in each hand, bring curved edges together as they feed under the presser foot while stitching a ¼" seam. Repeat to sew all CD sets. Press seam towards D.

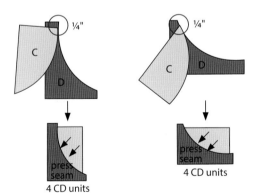

Square Up the Units

6. Square up the AB units to 4" x 4". Position WCR on blocks as shown with blue dots on curved seams or point. Trim side and top. Rotate block and align trimmed edges with 4" marks and trim remaining fabric. Repeat for all AB units.

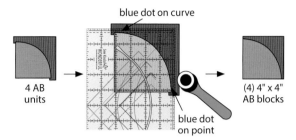

7. Square up the ABB units to 4" x 4". Position WCR on blocks as shown with blue dots on curved seam or point. Trim side and top. Rotate block and align trimmed edges with 4" marks and trim remaining fabric. Repeat for all ABB blocks.

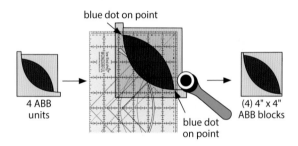

8. Square up the CD units to 2¼" x 4". Position WCR on block as shown with the blue dot on curved seam and 2" mark on curved seam. Trim side and top. Rotate block and align trimmed edges with 2¼" and 4" marks and trim remaining fabric.

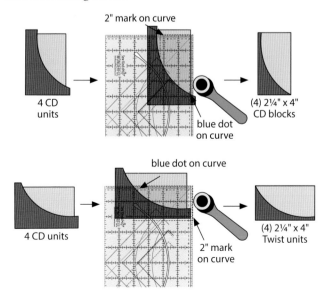

Assemble the Block

9. Lay out units as shown. Sew center blocks and side units together first as shown in boxes. Press seams. Sew to form rows. Press seams. Sew rows together. Press seams.

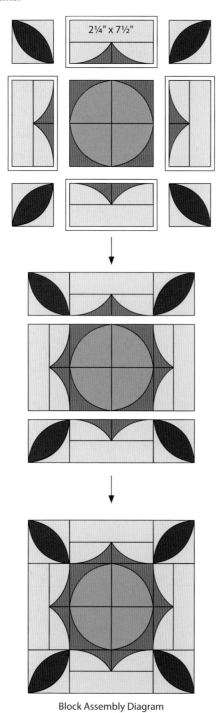

Block Assembly Diagram

Alternate Color & Layout Options

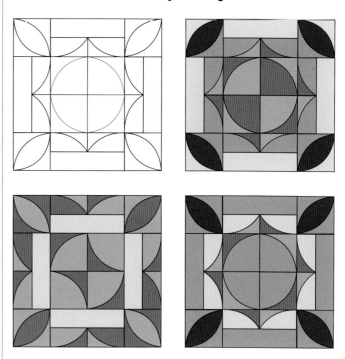

Custom Quilting Detail

Mod Sampler Quilt, see page 85

Block 11 - Basket

Unfinished block size: 14½" x 14½"

MATERIALS FOR 1 BLOCK
✢ 1 each 10" x 10" flower focus fabric in yellow, green, and light green
✢ 1 each 8" x 20" basket focus fabric in black and orange
✢ ⅓ yard neutral background fabric
✢ Wonder Curve Ruler™ (WCR)

GENERAL CUTTING
From yellow flower focus fabric, cut:
✢ (2) 4¼" x 4¼" squares
✢ (2) 5" x 5" squares

From each green and light flower focus fabric, cut:
✢ (1) 5" x 5" square
✢ (1) 2¾" x 4½" rectangle

From black basket focus fabric, cut:
✢ (2) 5" x 5" squares
✢ (1) 2¼" x 14½" rectangle
✢ (1) 2¼" x 7½" rectangle

From orange basket focus fabric, cut:
✢ (2) 4¼" x 4¼" squares
✢ (1) 4" x 7½" rectangle

From background fabric, cut:
✢ (4) 5¾" x 5¾" squares
✢ (2) 2¾" x 4½" rectangles
✢ (2) 4" x 4" squares
✢ (2) 2¼" x 4" rectangles

Cut the Curves

Refer to pages 13 and 14 to cut the following Shimmer, Antler, and Twist curves with the WCR.

Yellow flower focus fabric:
Shimmer A
From two 4¼" x 4¼" squares, cut two A curves.

Antler F
From two 5" x 5" squares, cut one F curve right side up (RSU) and one F curve right side down (RSD).

Green flower focus fabric:
Shimmer A & B
From 5" x 5" square, cut one B curve; discard the A curve piece.

Twist C
From 2¾" x 4½" rectangle, cut one C curve RSU.

Light green flower focus fabric:
Shimmer A & B
From 5" x 5" square, cut one B curve; discard the A curve piece.

Twist C
From 2¾" x 4½" rectangle, cut one C curve RSD.

Black basket focus fabric:
Antler F
From two 5" x 5" squares, cut one F curve RSU and one F curve RSD.

Orange basket focus fabric:
Shimmer A
From two 4¼" x 4¼" squares, cut two A curves.

Background fabric:
Shimmer B
From four 5¾" x 5¾" squares cut in half diagonally, cut eight B curves.

Twist C
From two 2¾" x 4½" rectangles, cut one C curve RSU and one C curve RSD.

Sew the Curves

1. Lay out the following sets:

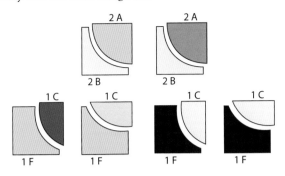

2. Position A on B, right sides together (RST), with ¼" of B extending beyond A as shown. Holding one piece in each hand, bring curved edges together as they feed under the presser foot while stitching a ¼" seam (see page 12). Repeat to sew all AB sets. Press seam towards A.

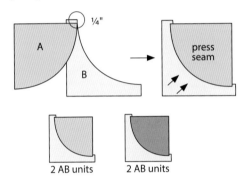

3. Working with the two AB yellow flower and background units, position AB under WCR with curved seam aligned with the blue curved line as shown. Cut in the curve cut-out. Discard small piece.

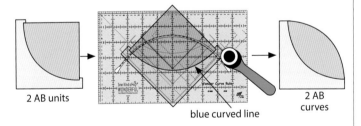

4. Lay out AB trimmed units and one light green B curve piece and one green B curve piece. Position AB on B, RST, with ¼" tail of B extending beyond AB as shown. Sew curved seam to make ABB unit. Press seam towards B. Repeat for remaining set.

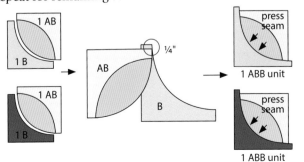

5. Position C on F, RST, as shown, matching ends or leaving a ¾" tail as indicated. Sew curved seam. Press seam towards F.

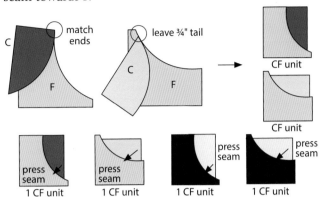

6. Position WCR on four CF units as shown with circle on the V line on curved seam. Cut in the curve cut-out. Discard small piece. Repeat for all CF units.

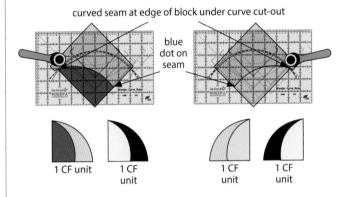

7. Position CF on B, RST, as shown, leaving a ¼" tail. Sew the curved seam to make CFB block. Press seam towards B.

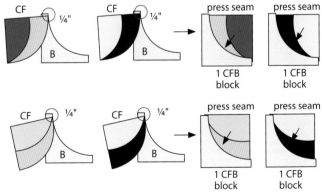

Square Up the Units

8. Square up the AB units to 4" x 4". Position WCR on blocks as shown with the blue dots on curved seam. Trim side and top. Rotate block and align trimmed edges with 4" marks and trim remaining fabric. Repeat for all AB blocks.

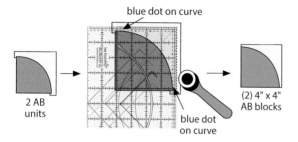

9. Square up the ABB units to 4" x 4". Position WCR on blocks as shown with the blue dots on curved points. Trim side and top. Rotate block and align trimmed edges with 4" marks and trim remaining fabric. Repeat for all ABB blocks.

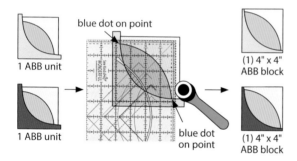

10. Square up the CFB block to 4" x 4". Position WCR on blocks as shown with blue dots on curved seams and points as shown. Trim side and top. Rotate block and align trimmed edges with 4" marks and trim remaining fabric. Repeat for all CFB blocks.

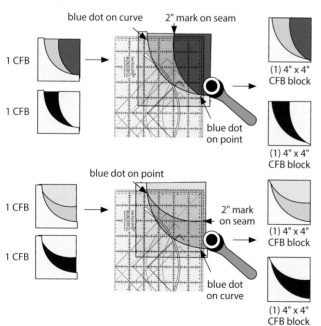

Assemble the Block

11. Lay out units as shown. Sew to form rows. Press seams open. Sew rows together. Press seams open.

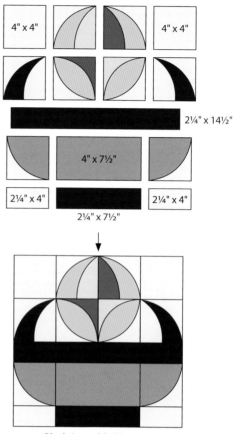

Block Assembly Diagram

Alternate Color & Layout Options

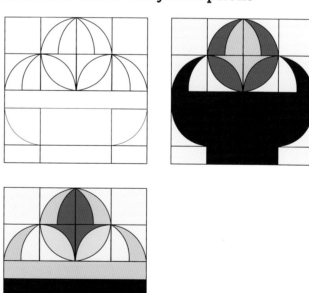

Favorite Things Quilt,
see page 93

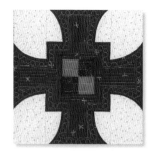

Block 12 - Clubhouse

Unfinished block size: 14½" x 14½"

MATERIALS FOR 1 BLOCK
+ 1 fat quarter focus fabric in blue
+ 1 each 5" x 5" fuchsia and orange fabric for center
+ 1 fat eighth neutral background fabric
+ Wonder Curve Ruler™ (WCR)

GENERAL CUTTING
From blue focus fabric, cut:
+ (8) 5" x 5" squares
+ (4) 2¼" x 4" rectangles
+ (4) 2¼" x 2¼" squares
From each fuchsia and orange fabric, cut:
+ (4) 2¼" x 2¼" squares
From background fabric, cut:
+ (4) 4" x 4" squares
+ (8) 2¾" x 4½" rectangles

Cut the Curves
Refer to page 14 to cut the following Antler and Twist curves with WCR.

Blue focus fabric:
Antler F
From eight 5" x 5" squares, cut four F curves right side up (RSU) and four F curves right side down (RSD).

4 F cut RSU   4 F cut RSD

Background fabric:
Twist C
From eight 2¾" x 4½" rectangles, cut four C curves RSU and four C curves RSD.

4 C cut RSU   4 C cut RSD

Sew the Curves
1. Lay out the following sets:

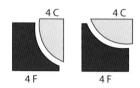

4 C   4 C
4 F   4 F

2. Position C on F, right sides together (RST), as shown matching ends or leaving a ¾" tail as indicated. Sew curved seam (see page 12). Press seam towards F.

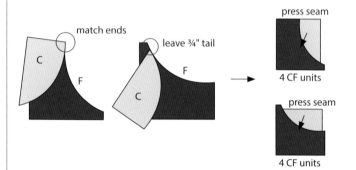

match ends   leave ¾" tail   press seam

C   F   F   4 CF units

C   press seam

4 CF units

Square Up the Units
3. Square up the CF units to 4" x 4". Position WCR on blocks as shown with the blue dots on curved seams. Trim side and top. Rotate block and align trimmed edges with 4" marks and trim remaining fabric. Repeat for all CF units.

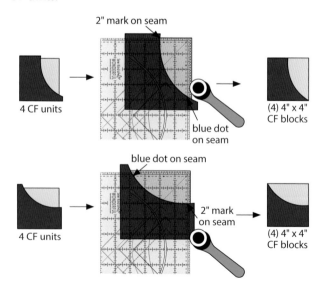

2" mark on seam

4 CF units   (4) 4" x 4" CF blocks

blue dot on seam

blue dot on seam

4 CF units   2" mark on seam   (4) 4" x 4" CF blocks

Sew Center Units

4. Lay out the center square pieces as shown. Sew to form rows. Press seams. Sew rows together. Repeat to make four center units with assorted fuchsia or orange fabrics.

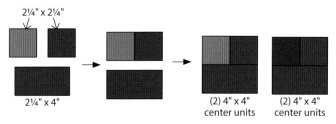

2¼" x 2¼"

2¼" x 4"

(2) 4" x 4" center units

(2) 4" x 4" center units

Assemble the Block

5. Lay out block units as shown. Sew to form rows. Press seams. Sew rows together, then press seams.

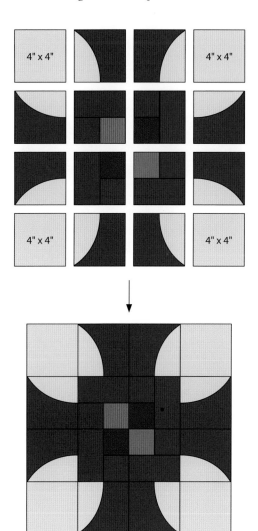

4" x 4"

4" x 4"

4" x 4"

4" x 4"

Block Assembly Diagram

Alternate Color & Layout Options

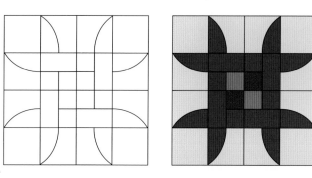

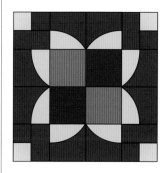

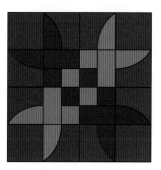

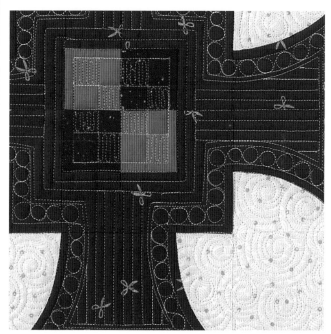

Custom Quilting Detail

Block 13 - Reflection

Unfinished block size: 14½" x 14½"

MATERIALS FOR 1 BLOCK
✛ 1 each fat eighth focus fabric in orange and red
✛ 1 each 12" x 20" background fabric in aqua and teal
✛ Wonder Curve Ruler™ (WCR)

GENERAL CUTTING
From orange focus fabric, cut:
✛ (3) 5¾" x 5¾" squares
From red focus fabric, cut:
✛ (6) 4¼" x 4¼" squares
From aqua background fabric, cut:
✛ (6) 4¼" x 4¼" squares
✛ (2) 5" x 5" squares
From teal background fabric, cut:
✛ (3) 5¾" x 5¾" squares
✛ (2) 5" x 5" squares

Cut the Curves

Refer to page 13 to cut the following Shimmer curves with the WCR.

Orange focus fabric:
Shimmer B
From three 5¾" x 5¾" squares cut in half diagonally, cut six B curves.

6 B

Red focus fabric:
Shimmer A
From six 4¼" x 4¼" squares, cut six A curves.

6 A

Aqua focus fabric:
Shimmer A
From six 4¼" x 4¼" squares, cut six A curves.

6 A

Teal focus fabric:
Shimmer B
From three 5¾" x 5¾" squares cut in half diagonally, cut six B curves.

6 B

Sew the Curves

1. Lay out the following sets:

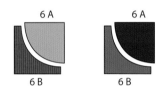

2. Position A on B, right sides together (RST), with ¼" of B extending beyond A as shown. Holding one piece in each hand, bring curved edges together as they feed under the presser foot while stitching a ¼" seam (see page 12). Repeat to sew all AB sets. Press seam towards A.

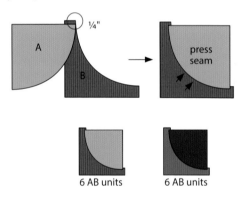

Make Half-Square Triangles

3. Make four half-square triangle (HST) blocks. Draw a line diagonally on wrong side of two 5" x 5" aqua squares. Layer, RST, with two 5" x 5" teal squares. Sew ¼" from drawn line on each side. Cut in half on drawn line. Press open.

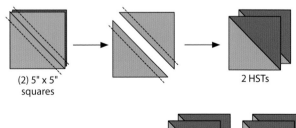

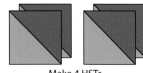

Make 4 HSTs

Square Up the Units

4. Square up the AB units to 4" x 4". Position WCR on blocks as shown with the blue dots on curved seams. Trim side and top. Rotate block and align trimmed edges with 4" marks and trim remaining fabric. Repeat for all AB units.

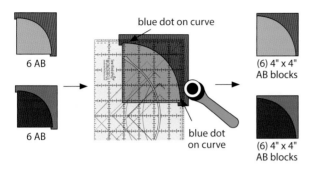

blue dot on curve

6 AB

6 AB

blue dot on curve

(6) 4" x 4" AB blocks

(6) 4" x 4" AB blocks

5. Square up all four HSTs to 4" x 4".

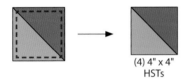

(4) 4" x 4" HSTs

Assemble the Block

6. Lay out units as shown. Sew to form rows. Press seams open. Sew rows together, then press seams open.

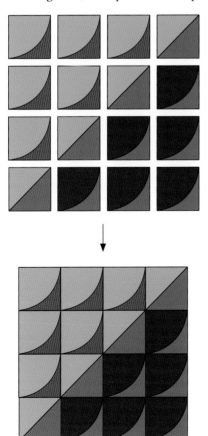

Block Assembly Diagram

Alternate Color & Layout Options

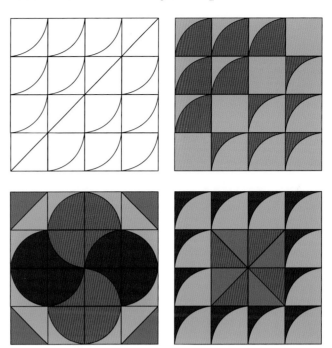

Custom Quilting Detail

Block 14 - Whirligig

Unfinished block size: 14½" x 14½"

MATERIALS FOR 1 BLOCK
+ 1 fat quarter focus fabic in mauve
+ (1) 12" x 20" focus fabric in orange
+ 1 each 10" x 10" focus fabric in white and gold
+ (1) 12" x 20" neutral background fabric
+ Wonder Curve Ruler™ (WCR)

GENERAL CUTTING

From mauve focus fabric, cut:
+ (8) 5" x 5" squares
+ (2) 5¾" x 5¾" squares

From orange focus fabric, cut:
+ (8) 2¾" x 4½" rectangles
+ (2) 5¾" x 5¾" squares

From white focus fabric, cut:
+ (4) 5" x 5" squares

From gold focus fabric, cut:
+ (4) 2¾" x 4½" rectangles

From background fabric, cut:
+ (4) 4¼" x 4¼" squares
+ (4) 5¾" x 5¾" squares

Cut the Curves

Refer to pages 13 and 14 to cut the following Antler, Shimmer, and Twist curves with the WCR.

Mauve focus fabric:
Antler F
From eight 5" x 5" squares, cut eight F curves right side up (RSU).

Shimmer B
From two 5¾" x 5¾" squares cut in half diagonally, cut four B curves.

Orange focus fabric:
Twist C
From eight 2¾" x 4½" rectangles, cut eight C curves RSU.

Shimmer B
From two 5¾" x 5¾" squares cut in half diagonally, cut four B curves.

White focus fabric:
Antler F
From four 5" x 5" squares, cut four F curves right side down (RSD).

Gold focus fabric:
Twist C
From four 2¾" x 4½" rectangles, cut four C curves RSD.

Background fabric:
Shimmer A
From four 4¼" x 4¼" squares, cut four A curves.

Shimmer B
From four 5¾" x 5¾" squares cut in half diagonally, cut eight B curves.

Sew the Curves

1. Lay out the following sets:

2. Position A on B, RST, with ¼" of B extending beyond A as shown. Holding one piece in each hand, bring curved edges together as they feed under the presser foot while stitching a ¼" seam (see page 12). Repeat to sew all AB sets. Press seam towards B.

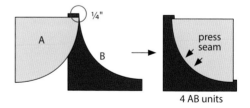

3. Position C on F, RST, as shown, matching ends or leaving a ¾" tail as indicated. Sew curved seam. Press seam towards F.

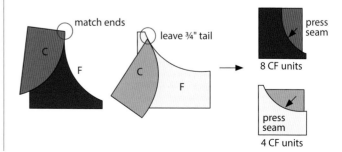

4. Position WCR on CF unit as shown with circle on V line on curved seam. Cut in the curve cut-out. Discard small piece cut off. Repeat for all CF units.

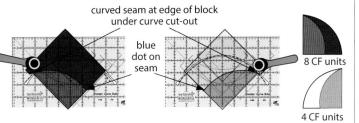

5. Position CF on B background, RST, as shown, leaving a ¼" tail. Sew the curved seam to make CFB block. Press seam towards B.

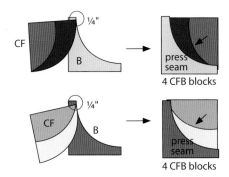

Square Up the Units

6. Square up the AB units to 4" x 4". Position WCR on blocks as shown with the blue dots on curved seams. Trim side and top. Rotate block and align trimmed edges with 4" marks and trim remaining fabric. Repeat for all AB units.

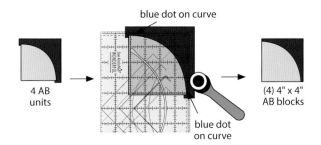

7. Square up CFB blocks to 4" x 4". Position WCR on blocks as shown with the blue dots on curved seam and point. Trim side and top. Rotate block and align trimmed edges with 4" marks and trim remaining fabric. Repeat for all CFB units.

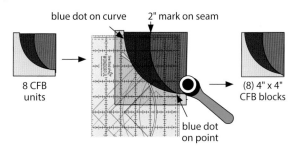

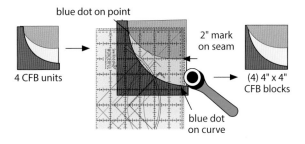

Assemble the Block

8. Lay out units as shown. Sew to form rows. Press seams open. Sew rows together, then press seams open.

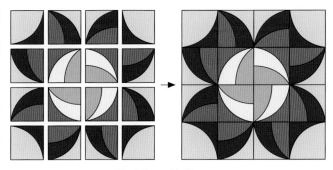

Block Assembly Diagram

Alternate Color & Layout Options

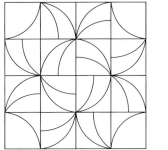
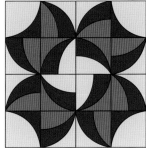

Block 15 - S.E.W.N.

Unfinished block size: 14½" x 14½"

MATERIALS FOR 1 BLOCK
+ (1) 12" x 12" focus fabric in orange
+ (1) 6" x 6" focus fabric in aqua
+ 1 fat quarter neutral background fabric
+ Wonder Curve Ruler™ (WCR)

GENERAL CUTTING
From orange focus fabric, cut:
+ (8) 2¾" x 2¾" squares
+ (2) 5¾" x 5¾" squares
From aqua focus fabric, cut:
+ (8) 1¾" x 1¾" squares
From background fabric cut:
+ (4) 4¼" x 4¼" squares
+ (12) 4" x 4" squares

Cut the Curves
Refer to page 13 to cut the following Shimmer curves with the WCR.

Peach focus fabric:
Shimmer B
From two 5¾" x 5¾" squares cut in half diagonally, cut four B curves.

Background fabric:
Shimmer A
From four 4¼" x 4¼" squares, cut four A curves.

Sew the Curves
1. Lay out the following sets:

2. Position A on B, right sides together (RST), with ¼" of B extending beyond A. Holding one piece in each hand, bring curved edges together as they feed under the presser foot while stitching a ¼" seam (see page 12). Repeat to sew all AB sets. Press seam towards B.

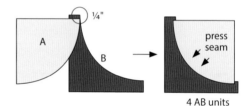

Square Up the Units
3. Square up the AB units to 4" x 4". Position WCR on blocks as shown with the blue dots on curved seam. Trim side and top. Rotate block and align trimmed edges with 4" marks and trim remaining fabric. Repeat for all AB units.

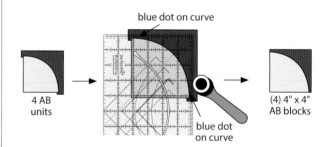

Sew Snowball Corners

4. Make a snowball corner on one corner of each of eight 4" background squares. Draw diagonal line on wrong side of the eight 1¾" aqua squares. Position on 4" square as shown. Sew on drawn line. Trim ¼" from sew line. Press open.

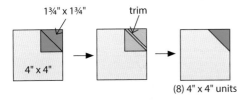

5. Make snowball corners on a corner adjacent to the aqua corners on the eight 4" x 4" units. Draw diagonal line on wrong side of the eight 2¾" orange squares. Position on 4" x 4" unit as shown. Sew on drawn line. Trim ¼" from sew line. Press open.

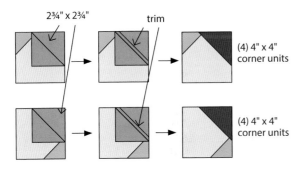

Custom Quilting Detail

Assemble the Block

6. Lay out units as shown. Sew to form rows. Press seams open. Sew rows together. Press seams open.

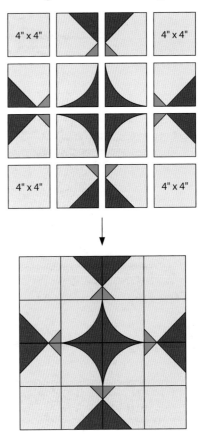

Block Assembly Diagram

Alternate Color & Layout Options

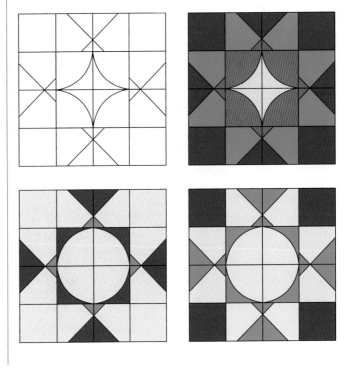

Block 16 - Bungalow

Unfinished block size: 14½" x 14½"

MATERIALS FOR 1 BLOCK
✢ 1 fat quarter house fabric in yellow
✢ (1) 5" x 20" roof fabric in black
✢ 1 each 5" x 10" accent fabric in pink, light gray, and blue
✢ (1) 3" x 3" accent fabric in brown
✢ (1) 5" x 20" neutral background fabric
✢ Wonder Curve Ruler™ (WCR)

GENERAL CUTTING
From yellow house fabric, cut:
✢ (1) 4" x 14½" rectangle
✢ (4) 2¼" x 5¾" rectangles
✢ (2) 3½" x 5" rectangles
From black roof fabric, cut:
✢ (1) 4¼" x 4¼" square
✢ (1) 4" x 11" rectangle
From pink accent fabric, cut:
✢ (2) 2¾" x 4½" rectangles for curtains
From light gray accent fabric, cut:
✢ (2) 3½" x 5" rectangles for window
✢ (1) 2¼" x 4" rectangle for window
From brown accent fabric, cut:
✢ (1) 2¼" x 2¼" square for chimney
From blue accent fabric, cut:
✢ (2) 2¾" x 4½" rectangles for door
✢ (1) 2¼" x 4" rectangle for door
From background fabric, cut:
✢ (1) 5" x 5" square
✢ (1) 2¼" x 11" rectangle
✢ (1) 2¼" x 2¼" square

Cut the Curves
Refer to pages 13 and 14 to cut the following Twist and Shimmer curves with the WCR.

Yellow house fabric:
Twist D
From two 3½" x 5" rectangles, cut one D curve right side up (RSU) and one D curve right side down (RSD).

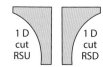

Black roof fabric:
Shimmer A
From the 4¼" x 4¼" square, cut one A curve.

Pink curtain fabric:
Twist C
From two 2¾" x 4½" rectangles, cut one C curve RSU and one C curve RSD.

Blue door fabric:
Twist C
From two 2¾" x 4½" rectangles, cut one C curve RSU and one C curve RSD.

Light gray window fabric:
Twist D
From two 3½" x 5" rectangles, cut one D curve RSU and one D curve RSD.

Background fabric:
Shimmer B
From 5" x 5" square, cut one B curve.

Sew the Curves:

1. Lay out the following sets:

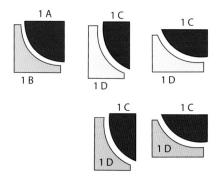

2. Position A on B, right sides together (RST), with ¼" of B extending beyond A as shown. Holding one piece in each hand, bring curved edges together as they feed under the presser foot while stitching a ¼" seam (see page 12). Repeat to sew all AB sets. Press seam towards A.

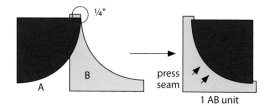

3. Position C on D, RST, with ¼" of D extending beyond C as shown. Holding one piece in each hand, bring curved edges together as they feed under the presser foot while stitching a ¼" seam. Repeat to sew all CD sets. Press seam towards C.

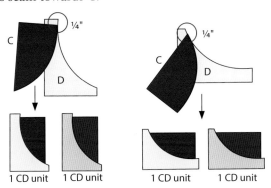

Square Up the Units

4. Square up the AB units to 4" x 4". Position WCR on blocks as shown with the blue dots on curved seam. Trim side and top. Rotate block and align trimmed edges with 4" marks and trim remaining fabric. Repeat for all AB units.

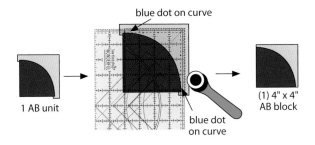

5. Square up the CD units to 2¼" x 4". Position WCR on block as shown with the blue dot on curved seam and 2" mark on curved seam. Trim side and top. Rotate block and align trimmed edges with 2¼" and 4" marks and trim remaining fabric.

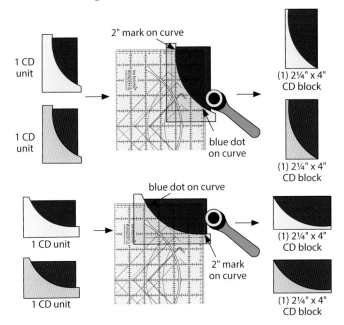

Assemble the Block

6. Lay out units as shown. Sew dashed sections together first. Press seams open. Sew to form rows. Press seams open. Sew rows together, then press seams open.

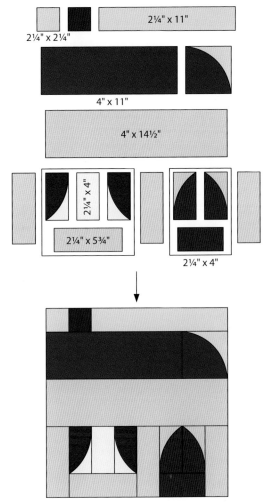

Block Assembly Diagram

Alternate Color & Layout Options

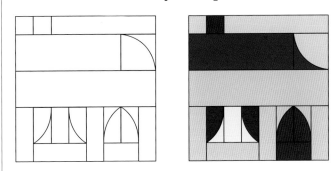

Block 17 - Rolling Stone

Unfinished block size: 14½" x 14½"

MATERIALS FOR 1 BLOCK
✧ (1) 6" x 20" focus fabric in aqua
✧ (1) 10" x 10" focus fabric in orange
✧ (1) 6" x 12" focus fabric in dark orange
✧ 1 fat quarter neutral background fabric
✧ Wonder Curve Ruler™ (WCR)

GENERAL CUTTING
From aqua focus fabric, cut:
✧ (8) 2¾" x 4½" rectangles

From orange focus fabric, cut:
✧ (4) 4¼" x 4¼" squares

From dark orange focus fabric, cut:
✧ (2) 5¾" x 5¾" squares

From background fabric, cut:
✧ (8) 5" x 5" squares
✧ (2) 5¾" x 5¾" squares
✧ (4) 4" x 4" squares

Cut the Curves:

Refer to pages 13 and 14 to cut the following Twist, Shimmer, and Antler curves with WCR.

Aqua focus fabric:
Twist C
From eight 2¾" x 4½" rectangles, cut four C curves right side up (RSU) and four C curves right side down (RSD).

4 C cut RSU   4 C cut RSD

Orange focus fabric:
Shimmer A
From four 4¼" x 4¼" squares, cut four A curves.

4 A

Dark orange focus fabric:
Shimmer B
From two 5¾" x 5¾" squares cut in half diagonally, cut four B curves.

4 B

Background fabric:
Antler F
From eight 5" x 5" squares, cut four F curves RSU and four F curves RSD.

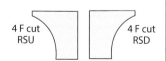

4 F cut RSU   4 F cut RSD

Shimmer B
From two 5¾" x 5¾" squares cut in half diagonally, cut four B curves.

4 B

Sew the Curves

1. Lay out the following sets:

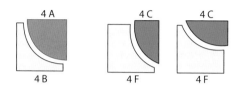

4 A / 4 B   4 C / 4 F   4 C / 4 F

2. Position A on B, right sides together (RST), with ¼" of B extending beyond A as shown. Holding one piece in each hand, bring curved edges together as they feed under the presser foot while stitching a ¼" seam (see page 12). Repeat to sew all AB sets. Press seam towards A.

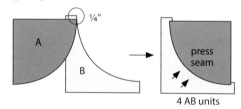

4 AB units

3. Working with the four AB units, position AB under WCR with curved seam aligned with the blue curved line as shown. Cut in the curve cut-out. Discard small piece.

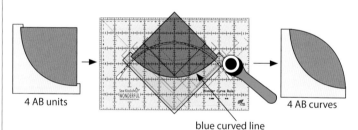

4 AB units   4 AB curves

blue curved line

4. Lay out trimmed AB units and four orange B curves as shown. Position AB on B, RST, with a ¼" tail of B extending beyond AB. Sew curved seam to make ABB unit. Press seam towards B. Repeat for remaining set.

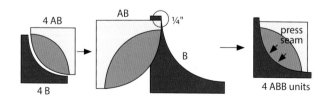

4 AB   AB   4 B   4 ABB units

5. Position C on F, RST, as shown, matching ends or leaving a ¾" tail as indicated. Sew curved seam. Press seam towards F.

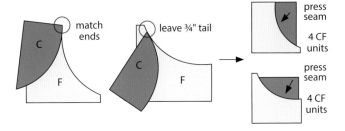

Square Up the Units

6. Square up the ABB units to 4" x 4". Position WCR on blocks as shown with the blue dots on points. Trim side and top. Rotate block and align trimmed edges with 4" marks and trim remaining fabric. Repeat for all ABB units.

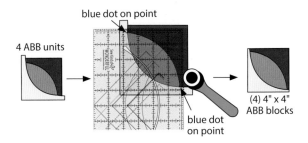

7. Square up the CF unit to 4" x 4". Position WCR on blocks as shown with the blue dots on curved seams. Trim side and top. Rotate block and align trimmed edges with 4" marks and trim remaining fabric. Repeat for all CF units.

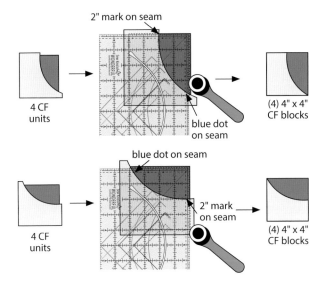

Assemble the Block

8. Lay out units as shown. Sew to form rows. Press seams open. Sew rows together, then press seams open.

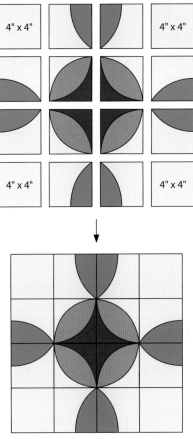

Block Assembly Diagram

Alternate Color & Layout Options

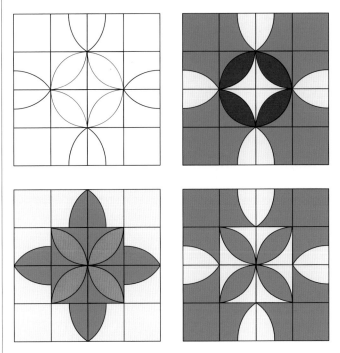

Block 18 - Star Shine

Unfinished block size: 14½" x 14½"

MATERIALS FOR 1 BLOCK
+ (1) 5" x 10" focus fabric in black
+ 1 fat quarter focus fabric in blue
+ (1) 12" x 20" focus fabric in dark blue
+ (1) 7" x 20" background fabric in white
+ Wonder Curve Ruler™ (WCR)

GENERAL CUTTING
From black focus fabric, cut:
+ (2) 5" x 5" squares
From blue focus fabric, cut:
+ (2) 5" x 5" squares
+ (8) 4¼" x 4¼" squares
From dark blue focus fabric, cut:
+ (6) 5¾" x 5¾" squares
From white background fabric, cut:
+ (4) 4¼" x 4¼" squares
+ (4) 2¼" x 2¼" squares

Cut the Curves

Refer to page 13 to cut the following Shimmer curves with the WCR.

Blue focus fabric:
Shimmer A
From eight 4¼" x 4¼" squares, cut eight A curves.

8 A

Dark blue focus fabric:
Shimmer B
From six 5¾" x 5¾" squares cut in half diagonally, cut twelve B curves.

12 B

White background fabric:
Shimmer A
From four 4¼" x 4¼" squares, cut four A curves.

4 A

Sew the Curves

1. Lay out the following sets:

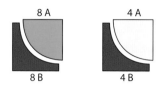

2. Position A on B, right sides together (RST), with ¼" of B extending beyond A as shown. Holding one piece in each hand, bring curved edges together as they feed under the presser foot while stitching a ¼" seam (see page 12). Repeat to sew all AB sets. Press seam towards A.

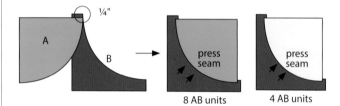

Make Half-Square Triangles

3. Make four half-square triangle (HST) units. Draw a line diagonally on wrong side of two 5" blue squares. Layer, RST, with two 5" black squares. Sew ¼" from drawn line on each side. Cut in half on drawn line. Press open.

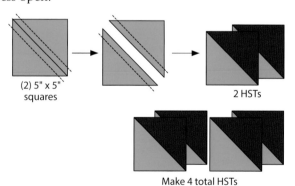

Make 4 total HSTs

Square Up the Units

4. Square up the AB units to 4" x 4". Position WCR on blocks as shown with the blue dots on curved seams. Trim side and top. Rotate block and align trimmed edges with 4" marks and trim remaining fabric. Repeat for all AB units.

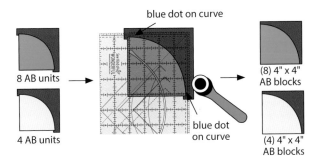

5. Square up all four HSTs to 4" x 4".

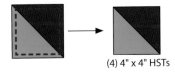

(4) 4" x 4" HSTs

Sew Snowball Corners

6. Make white snowball corners on all four HSTs. Draw a diagonal line on wrong side of four 2¼" white squares. Position on HST as shown. Sew on drawn line. Trim ¼" from seam. Press open.

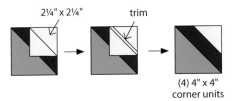

(4) 4" x 4" corner units

Assemble the Block

7. Lay out units as shown. Sew to form rows. Press seams open. Sew rows together, then press seams open.

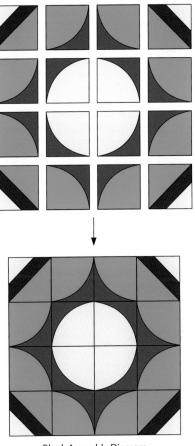

Block Assembly Diagram

Alternate Color & Layout Options

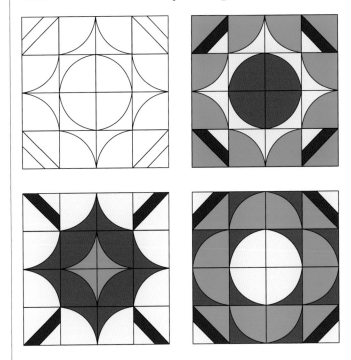

Block 19 - Flower Show

Unfinished block size: 14½" x 14½"

Cut the Curves

Refer to page 13 to cut the following Shimmer curves using the WCR.

Fuchsia flower focus fabric:
Shimmer A
From eight 4¼" x 4¼" squares, cut eight A curves.

4 A

Orange flower center fabric:
Shimmer B
From two 5¾" x 5¾" squares cut in half diagonally, cut four B curves.

4 B

Yellow flower center fabric:
Shimmer B
From two 5¾" x 5¾" squares cut in half diagonally, cut four B curves.

4 B

Green leaf fabric:
Shimmer A
From four 4¼" x 4¼" squares, cut four A curves.

4 A

Citrine leaf fabric:
Shimmer A
From four 4¼" x 4¼" squares, cut four A curves,

4 A

Background fabric:
Shimmer B
From twelve 5¾" x 5¾" squares cut in half diagonally, cut twelve B curves.

24B

Sew the Curves

1. Lay out the following sets:

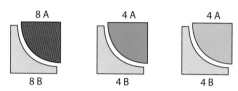

2. Position A on B, right sides together (RST), with ¼" of B extending beyond A. Holding one piece in each hand, bring curved edges together as they feed under the presser foot while stitching a ¼" seam (see page 12). Repeat to sew all AB sets. Press seam towards A.

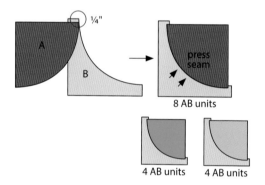

3. Working with the AB pink and background units only, position AB under WCR with curved seam aligned with the blue curved line as shown. Cut in the curve cut-out. Discard small piece. Repeat for remaining AB green and background and AB citrine and background units.

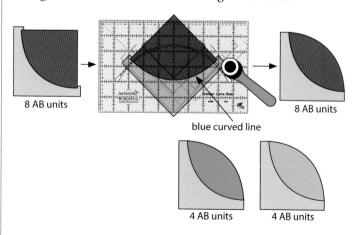

4. Lay out AB trimmed units and four orange B pieces, four yellow B pieces, and eight background B pieces as shown. Position AB on B, RST, with a ¼" tail of B extending beyond AB as shown. Sew curved seam to make ABB units. Press seam towards B. Repeat for remaining sets.

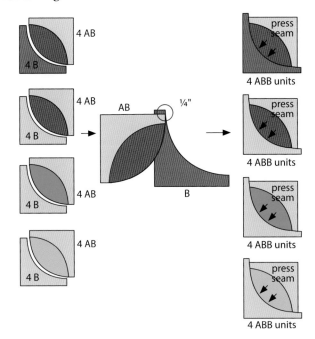

Square Up the Units

5. Square up the ABB units to 4" x 4". Position WCR on blocks as shown with the blue dots on points. Trim side and top. Rotate block and align trimmed edges with 4" marks and trim remaining fabric. Repeat for all ABB units.

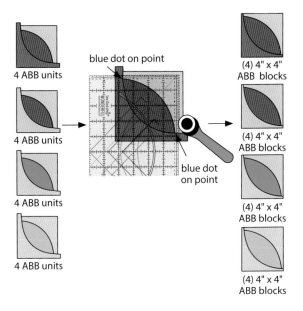

Assemble the Block

6. Lay out units as shown. Sew to form rows. Press seams open. Sew rows together, then press seams open.

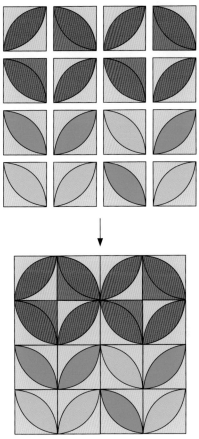

Block Assembly Diagram

Alternate Color & Layout Options

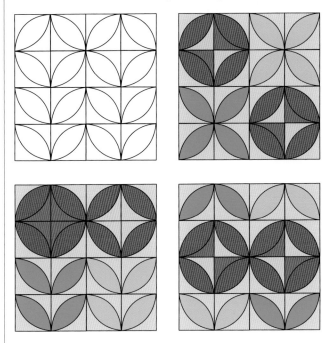

Block 20 - 4 Frogs

Unfinished block size: 14½" x 14½"

MATERIALS FOR 1 BLOCK
✛ 1 each 10" x 20" focus fabric in blue and navy
✛ 1 fat quarter neutral background fabric
✛ Wonder Curve Ruler™ (WCR)

GENERAL CUTTING
From each blue and navy focus fabric, cut:
✛ (4) 4¼" x 4¼" squares
✛ (2) 5" x 5" squares
From background fabric, cut:
✛ (4) 5¾" x 5¾" squares
✛ (4) 4" x 4" squares

Cut the Curves

Refer to page 13 to cut the following Shimmer curves with the WCR.

Blue focus fabric:
Shimmer A
From four 4¼" x 4¼" squares, cut four A curves.

Navy focus fabric:
Shimmer A
From four 4¼" x 4¼" squares, cut four A curves.

Background fabric:
Shimmer B
From four 5¾ x 5¾" squares cut in half diagonally, cut eight B curves.

Sew the Curves

1. Lay out the following sets:

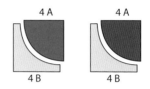

2. Position A on B, right sides together (RST), with ¼" of B extending beyond A as shown. Holding one piece in each hand, bring curved edges together as they feed under the presser foot while stitching a ¼" seam (see page 12). Repeat to sew all AB sets. Press seam towards A.

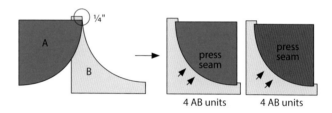

Make Half-Square Triangles

3. Make four half-square triangle (HST) units. Draw a line diagonally on wrong side of blue squares. Layer, RST, with two navy squares. Sew ¼" from drawn line on each side. Cut in half on drawn line. Press open.

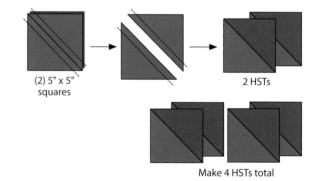

Square Up the Units

4. Square up the AB units to 4" x 4". Position WCR on blocks as shown with the blue dots on curved seams. Trim side and top. Rotate block and align trimmed edges with 4" marks and trim remaining fabric. Repeat for all AB units.

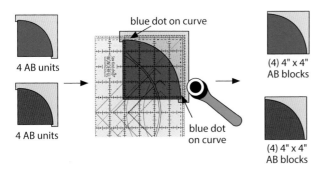

5. Square up all four HSTs blocks to 4" x 4".

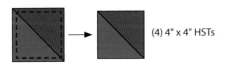

Assemble the Block

6. Lay out units as shown. Sew to form rows. Press seams open. Sew rows together, then press seams open.

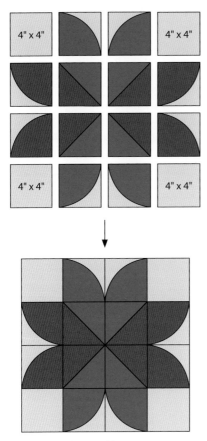

Block Assembly Diagram

Alternate Color & Layout Options

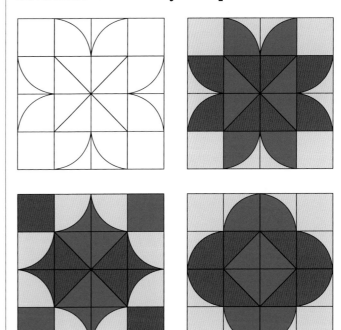

Custom Quilting Detail

Block 21 - Stair Stepper

Unfinished block size: 14½" x 14½"

MATERIALS FOR 1 BLOCK
✢ 1 each 5" x 15" focus fabric in blue and periwinkle
✢ (1) 5" x 20" focus fabric in teal
✢ (1) 12" x 12" focus fabric in gold
✢ (1) 8" x 12" neutral background fabric
✢ Wonder Curve Ruler™ (WCR)

GENERAL CUTTING
From blue and periwinkle focus fabric, cut:
✢ (3) 5" x 5" squares
From teal focus fabric, cut:
✢ (4) 4¼" x 4¼" squares
From gold focus fabric, cut:
✢ (4) 5¾" x 5¾" squares
From background fabric, cut:
✢ (6) 4" x 4" squares

Cut the Curves

Refer to page 13 to cut the following Shimmer curves with the WCR.

Teal focus fabric:
Shimmer A
From four 4¼" x 4¼" squares, cut four A curves.

4 A

Gold focus fabric:
Shimmer B
From four 5¾ x 5¾" squares cut in half diagonally, cut eight B curves.

8 B

Sew the curves

1. Lay out the following sets:

4 A

4 B

2. Position A on B, right sides together (RST), with ¼" of B extending beyond A as shown. Holding one piece in each hand, bring curved edges together as they feed under the presser foot while stitching a ¼" seam (see page 12). Repeat to sew all AB sets. Press seam towards A.

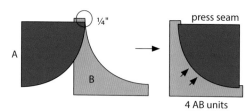

¼"   press seam

A

B

4 AB units

3. Working with four AB units, position AB under WCR with curved seam aligned with the blue curved line as shown. Cut in the curve cut-out. Discard small piece.

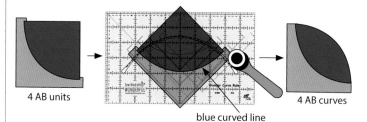

4 AB units   4 AB curves

blue curved line

4. Lay out AB trimmed units and four gold B pieces. Position AB on B, RST, with a ¼" tail of B extending beyond AB as shown. Sew curved seam to make ABB block. Press seam towards B. Repeat for remaining ABB units.

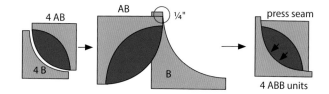

4 AB   AB   ¼"   press seam

4 B   B   4 ABB units

Make Half-Square Triangles

5. Make six half-square triangle (HST) units. Draw a line diagonally on wrong side of three 5" blue squares. Layer, RST, with three 5" periwinkle squares. Sew ¼" from drawn line on each side. Cut in half on drawn line. Press open.

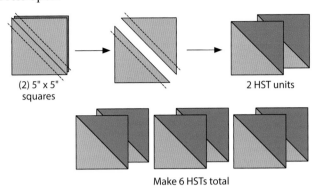

(2) 5" x 5" squares

2 HST units

Make 6 HSTs total

Square Up the Units

6. Square up the ABB units to 4" x 4". Position WCR on blocks as shown with the blue dots on points. Trim side and top. Rotate block and align trimmed edges with 4" marks and trim remaining fabric. Repeat for all ABB units.

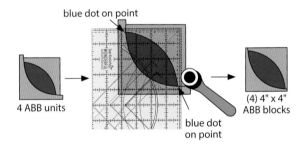

blue dot on point

4 ABB units

blue dot on point

(4) 4" x 4" ABB blocks

7. Square-up all six HST blocks to 4" x 4".

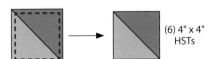

(6) 4" x 4" HSTs

Assemble the Block

8. Lay out units as shown. Sew to form rows. Press seams open. Sew rows together, then press seams open.

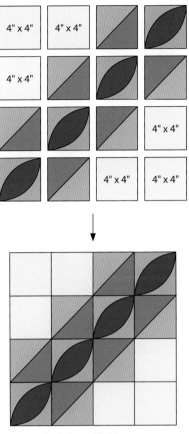

Block Assembly Diagram

Alternate Color & Layout Options

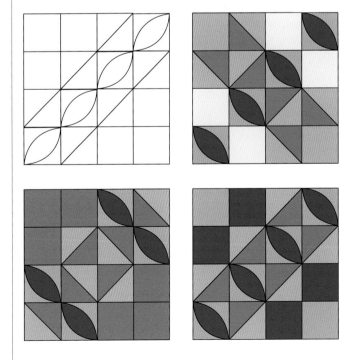

Block 22 - Checkers

Unfinished block size: 14½" x 14½"

MATERIALS FOR 1 BLOCK
✛ (1) 12" x 12" focus fabric in emerald green
✛ 1 each 5" x 10" focus fabric in black and sage
✛ 1 fat quarter neutral background fabric
✛ Wonder Curve Ruler™ (WCR)

GENERAL CUTTING
From emerald green focus fabric, cut:
✛ (4) 5¾" x 5¾" squares
From each black and sage focus fabric, cut:
✛ (8) 2¼" x 2¼" squares
From background fabric, cut:
✛ (8) 4¼" x 4¼" squares
✛ (4) 4" x 4" squares

Cut the Curves

Refer to page 13 to cut the following Shimmer curves with the WCR.

Emerald green focus fabric:
Shimmer B
From four 5¾" x 5¾" squares cut in half diagonally, cut eight B curves.

8 B

Background fabric:
Shimmer A
From eight 4¼" x 4¼" squares, cut eight A curves.

8 A

Sew the Curves

1. Lay out the following sets:

8 A

8 B

2. Position A on B, right sides together (RST), with ¼" of B extending beyond A as shown. Holding one piece in each hand, bring curved edges together as they feed under the presser foot while stitching a ¼" seam (see page 12). Repeat to sew all AB sets. Press seam towards B.

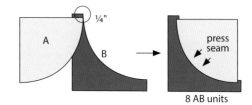

¼"

A

B

press seam

8 AB units

Square Up the Units

3. Square up the AB units to 4" x 4". Position WCR on blocks as shown with the blue dots on curved seams or points. Trim side and top. Rotate block and align trimmed edges with 4" marks and trim remaining fabric. Repeat for all AB units.

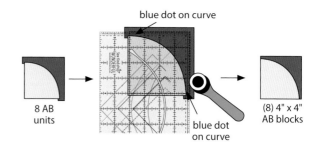

blue dot on curve

8 AB units

blue dot on curve

(8) 4" x 4" AB blocks

Sew the Center Units

4. Lay out black and sage 2¼" squares as shown. Sew to form rows. Press seams. Sew rows together. Repeat to make four center units.

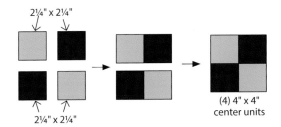

Assemble the Block

5. Lay out units as shown. Sew to form rows. Press seams. Sew rows together, then press seams.

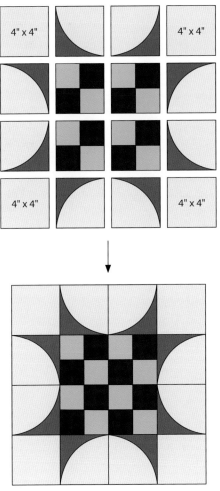

Block Assembly Diagram

Alternate Color & Layout Options

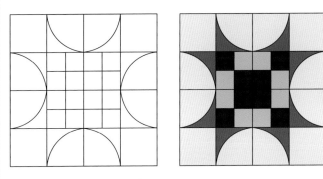

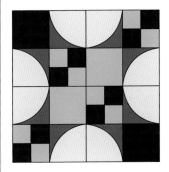
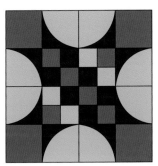

Custom Quilting Detail

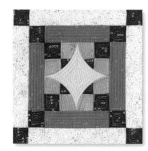

Block 23 - Chained

Unfinished block size: 14½" x 14½"

MATERIALS FOR 1 BLOCK
✛ (1) 5" x 20" focus fabric in red
✛ (1) 8 x 20" focus fabric in white
✛ (1) 5" x 15" focus fabric in blue
✛ (1) 5" x 10" focus fabric in light blue
✛ (1) 6" x 12" focus fabric in yellow
✛ Wonder Curve Ruler™ (WCR)

GENERAL CUTTING
From red focus fabric, cut:
✛ (12) 2¼" x 2¼" squares
✛ (4) 2½" x 2½" squares
From white fabric, cut:
✛ (4) 2¼" x 7½" rectangles
✛ (8) 2¼" x 2¼" squares
From blue focus fabric, cut:
✛ (4) 2¼" x 7½" rectangles
From light blue focus fabric, cut:
✛ (8) 2¼" x 2½" rectangles
From yellow focus fabric, cut:
✛ (2) 5¾" x 5¾" squares

Cut the Curves

Refer to page 13 to cut the following Shimmer curves with the WCR.

Yellow focus fabric:
Shimmer B
From two 5¾" x 5¾" squares cut in half diagonally, cut four B curves.

Sew 4-patch Units

1. Lay out red and white 2¼" square pieces as shown. Sew to form rows. Press seams. Sew rows together. Repeat to make four 4-patches.

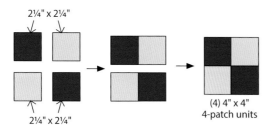

2. Lay out red and light blue pieces as shown with the larger 2½" red square in the upper left corner (X indicates the larger red patch). Sew to form rows. Press seams. Sew rows together. Repeat to make four 4-patch units.

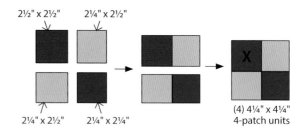

3. Cut A curves from 4-patch units. Position WCR on 4-patch as shown. Ensure patch marked with X is in correct orientation. Cut in the curve cut-out. Discard small piece. Repeat to cut four A 4-patch curves.

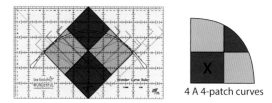

4 A 4-patch curves

Sew the Curves
4. Lay out the following sets:

5. Position A on B, right sides together (RST), with ¼" of B extending beyond A as shown. Holding one piece in each hand, bring curved edges together as they feed under the presser foot while stitching a ¼" seam (see page 12). Repeat to sew all AB sets. Press seam towards A.

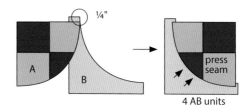

Square Up the Units

6. Square up the AB units to 4" x 4". Position WCR on blocks as shown with the blue dots on curved seams. Trim side and top. Rotate block and align trimmed edges with 4" marks and trim remaining fabric. Repeat for all AB units.

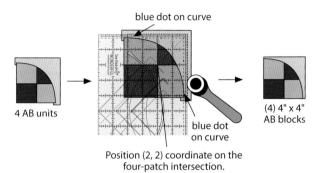

blue dot on curve

4 AB units

blue dot on curve

(4) 4" x 4" AB blocks

Position (2, 2) coordinate on the four-patch intersection.

Assemble the Block

7. Lay out units as shown. Sew boxed sections together first. Press seams. Sew to form rows. Press seams. Sew rows together, then press seams again.

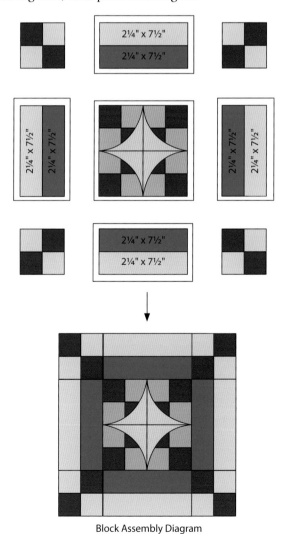

Block Assembly Diagram

Alternate Color & Layout Options

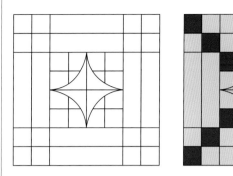

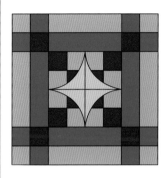
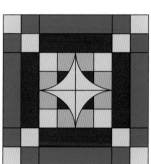

Custom Quilting Detail

Block 24 - Crossings

Unfinished block size: 14½" x 14½"

MATERIALS FOR 1 BLOCK
✛ 1 fat quarter focus fabric in dark orange
✛ 1 fat eighth accent fabric in orange
✛ (1) 6" x 12" accent fabric in aqua
✛ (1) 8" x 20" neutral background fabric
✛ Wonder Curve Ruler™ (WCR)

GENERAL CUTTING
From dark orange focus fabric, cut:
✛ (4) 5" x 5" squares
✛ (4) 4" x 4" squares
✛ (2) 5¾" x 5¾" squares
From orange accent fabric, cut:
✛ (8) 2¼" x 2¼" squares
✛ (4) 4¼" x 4¼" squares
From aqua accent fabric, cut:
✛ (2) 5¾" x 5¾" squares
From background fabric, cut
✛ (4) 5" x 5" squares
✛ (4) 2¼" x 2¼" squares

Cut the Curves

Refer to page 13 to cut the following Shimmer curves with the WRC.

Dark orange focus fabric:
Shimmer B
From two 5¾" x 5¾" squares cut in half diagonally, cut four B curves.

4 B

Orange accent fabric:
Shimmer A
From four 4¼" x 4¼" squares, cut four A curves.

4 A

Aqua accent fabric:
Shimmer B
From two 5¾" x 5¾" squares cut in half diagonally, cut four B curves.

4 B

Sew the Curves

1. Lay out the following sets:

4 A
4 B

2. Position A on B, right sides together (RST), with ¼" of B extending beyond A as shown. Holding one piece in each hand, bring curved edges together as they feed under the presser foot while stitching a ¼" seam (see page 12). Repeat to sew all AB sets. Press seam towards A.

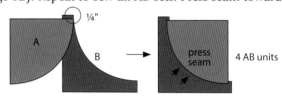

3. Working with the four AB units, position AB under WCR with curved seam aligned with the blue curved line as shown. Cut in the curve cut-out. Discard small piece.

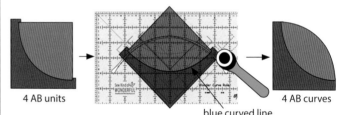

4. Lay out AB trimmed units and four aqua B pieces. Position AB on B, RST, with a ¼" tail of B extending beyond AB as shown. Sew curved seam to make ABB units. Press seam towards B.

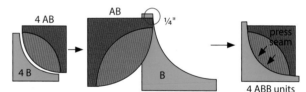

Sew Half-Square Triangle Units

5. Make four half-square triangle (HST) blocks. Draw a line diagonally on wrong side of two 5" background squares. Layer, RST, with two 5" dark orange squares. Sew ¼" from drawn line on each side. Cut in half on drawn line. Press open.

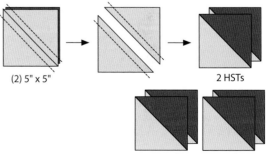

Make 8 HSTs total

Square Up the Units

6. Square up the ABB units to 4" x 4". Position WCR on blocks as shown with the blue dots on points. Trim side and top. Rotate block and align trimmed edges with 4" marks and trim remaining fabric. Repeat for all ABB units.

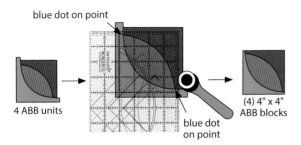

blue dot on point

4 ABB units

blue dot on point

(4) 4" x 4" ABB blocks

7. Square up all four HST units to 4" x 4".

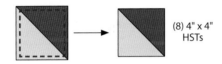

(8) 4" x 4" HSTs

Sew the Corner Units

8. Make four corner units. Lay out one 2¼" background square and two 2¼" orange squares as shown. Sew two together. Press seam open. Sew third piece as shown. Press seam open.

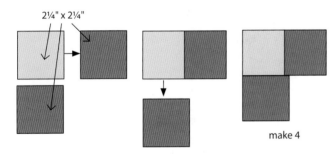

2¼" x 2¼"

make 4

9. Draw a diagonal line on wrong side of 3-piece units as shown. Position one 3-piece unit, RST, on a 4" orange square as shown. Sew on drawn line. Trim ¼" from seam. Press unit open. Repeat to make three more 3-piece HSTs.

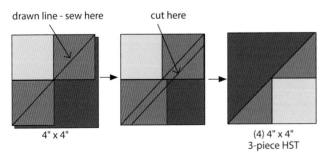

drawn line - sew here

cut here

4" x 4"

(4) 4" x 4" 3-piece HST

Assemble the Block

10. Lay out units as shown. Sew to form rows. Press seams open. Sew rows together. Press seams open.

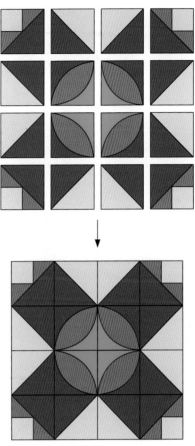

Block Assembly Diagram

Alternate Color & Layout Options

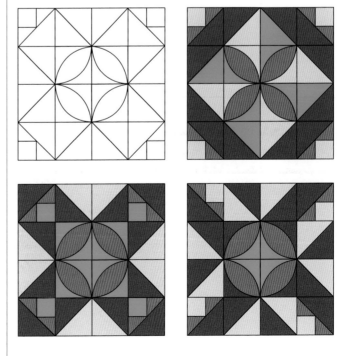

Block 25 - Tulip Time

Unfinished block size: 14½" x 14½"

MATERIALS FOR 1 BLOCK
✛ 1 each fat quarter focus fabric in light purple and dark purple
✛ (1) 5" x 10" accent focus fabric in blue
✛ (1) 5" x 5" accent focus fabric in pink
✛ (1) 10" x 14" background fabric
✛ Wonder Curve Ruler™ (WCR)

GENERAL CUTTING
From each light purple and dark purple focus fabric, cut:
✛ (4) 2¼" x 5¾" rectangles
✛ (4) 2¾" x 4½" rectangles
✛ (6) 2¼" x 2¼" squares
From blue accent fabric, cut:
✛ (8) 2¼" x 2¼" squares
From pink accent fabric, cut:
✛ (4) 2¼" x 2¼" squares
From background fabric, cut:
✛ (8) 3½" x 5" rectangles

Cut the Curves
Refer to page 14 to cut the following Twist curves with the WCR.

Light purple focus fabric:
Twist C
From four 2¾" x 4½" rectangles, cut two C curves right side up (RSU) and two C curves right side down (RSD).

2 C cut RSU   2 C cut RSD

Dark purple focus fabric:
Twist C
From four 2¾" x 4½" rectangles, cut two C curves RSU and two C curves RSD.

2 C cut RSU   2 C cut RSD

Background fabric:
Twist D
From eight 3½" x 5" rectangles, cut four C curves RSU and four C curves RSD.

4 C cut RSU   4 C cut RSD

Sew the Curves
1. Lay out the following sets:

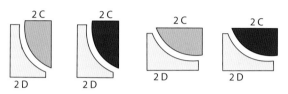
2 C   2 C   2 C   2 C
2 D   2 D   2 D   2 D

2. Position C on D, right sides together (RST), with ¼" of D extending beyond C as shown. Holding one piece in each hand, bring curved edges together as they feed under the presser foot while stitching a ¼" seam (see page 12). Repeat to sew all CD sets. Press seam towards C.

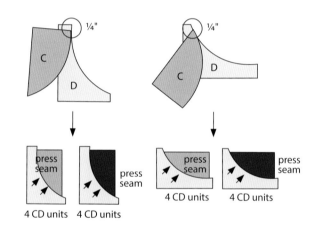

Square Up the Units

3. Square up the CD units to 2¼" x 4". Position WCR on block as shown with blue dot on curved seam and 2" mark on curved seam. Trim side and top. Rotate block and align trimmed edges with 2¼" and 4" marks and trim remaining fabric.

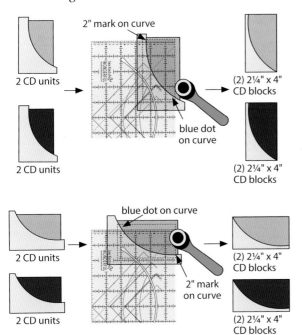

Sew the 4-patch Units

4. Lay out 2¼" square pieces in pink, blue, light purple, and dark purple as shown. Sew to form rows. Press seams. Sew rows together. Press seam. Make two pink, blue, and light purple 4-patch units; two pink, blue, and dark purple 4-patch units; and one light and dark purple 4-patch unit.

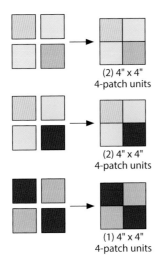

Assemble the Block

5. Lay out units as shown. Sew boxed sections together first. Press seams. Sew to form rows. Press seams. Sew rows together, then press seams.

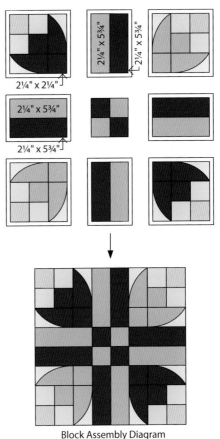

Block Assembly Diagram

Alternate Color & Layout Options

Block 26 - Moon Shine

Unfinished block size: 14½" x 14½"

MATERIALS FOR 1 BLOCK
✛ (1) 5" x 20" focus fabric in peach
✛ (1) 5" x 10" focus fabric in maroon
✛ 1 each fat quarter focus fabric in navy and pink
✛ (1) 5" x 5" focus fabric in blue
✛ Wonder Curve Ruler™ (WCR)

GENERAL CUTTING
From peach focus fabric, cut:
✛ (4) 4¼" x 4¼" squares
From maroon focus fabric, cut:
✛ (2) 5" x 5" squares
From blue focus fabric, cut:
✛ (4) 2¼" x 2¼" squares
From navy focus fabric, cut:
✛ (6) 5¾" x 5¾" squares
From pink focus fabric, cut:
✛ (8) 4¼" x 4¼" squares
✛ (2) 5" x 5" squares

Cut the Curves

Refer to page 13 to cut the following Shimmer curves with the WCR.

Peach focus fabric:
Shimmer A
From four 4¼" x 4¼" squares, cut four A curves.

4 A

Navy focus fabric:
Shimmer B
From six 5¾" x 5¾" squares cut in half diagonally, cut twelve B curves.

12 B

Pink focus fabric:
Shimmer A
From eight 4¼" x 4¼" squares, cut eight A curves.

8 A

Sew the Curves

1. Lay out the following sets:

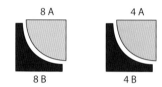

2. Position A on B, right sides together (RST), with ¼" of B extending beyond A as shown. Holding one piece in each hand, bring curved edges together as they feed under the presser foot while stitching a ¼" seam (see page 12). Repeat to sew all AB sets. Press seam towards A.

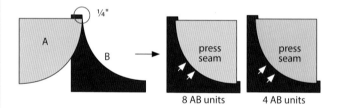

Make Half-Square Triangle Units

3. Make four half-square triangle (HST) blocks. Draw a line diagonally on wrong side of two 5" maroon squares. Layer, RST, with 5" pink squares. Sew ¼" from drawn line on each side. Cut in half on drawn line. Press open.

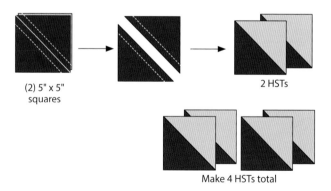

Square Up the Units

4. Square up the AB units to 4" x 4". Position WCR on blocks as shown with the blue dots on curved seams. Trim side and top. Rotate block and align trimmed edges with 4" marks and trim remaining fabric. Repeat for all AB units.

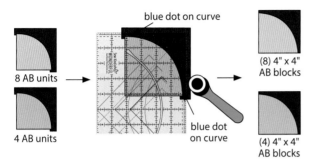

5. Square up all four HST units to 4" x 4".

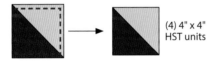

Sew Snowball Corners

6. Create snowball corners on each of the HSTs. Draw a diagonal line on wrong side of 2¼" blue squares. Position on HST as shown. Sew on drawn line. Trim ¼" from seam. Press open.

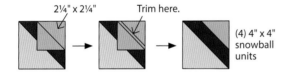

Assemble the Block

7. Lay out units as shown. Sew to form rows. Press seams open. Sew rows together. Press seams open.

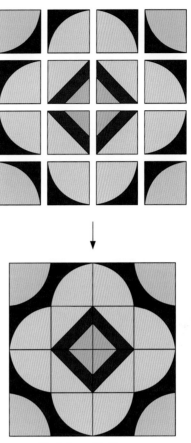

Block Assembly Diagram

Alternate Color & Layout Options

Block 27 - Bridges

Unfinished block size: 14½" x 14½"

<table>
<tr><td>

MATERIALS FOR 1 BLOCK
+ 1 each 5" x 20" focus fabric in aqua, light purple, blue, dark purple each
+ 1 fat quarter neutral background fabric
+ Wonder Curve Ruler™ (WCR)

GENERAL CUTTING
From each aqua, light purple, blue, dark purple focus fabric, cut:
+ (4) 4¼" x 4¼" squares
From background fabric, cut:
+ (8) 5¾" x 5¾" squares

</td></tr>
</table>

Cut the Curves

Refer to page 13 to cut the following Shimmer curves with the WRC.

Aqua focus fabric:
Shimmer A
From four 4¼" x 4¼" squares, cut four A curves.

4 A

Light purple focus fabric:
Shimmer A
From four 4¼" x 4¼" squares, cut four A curves.

4 A

Dark purple focus fabric:
Shimmer A
From four 4¼" x 4¼" squares, cut four A curves.

4 A

Blue focus fabric:
Shimmer A
From four 4¼" x 4¼" squares, cut four A curves.

4 A

Background fabric:
Shimmer B
From eight 5¾" x 5¾" squares cut in half diagonally, cut sixteen B curves.

16 B

Sew the Curves

1. Lay out the following sets:

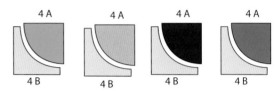
4 A   4 A   4 A   4 A
4 B   4 B   4 B   4 B

2. Position A on B, right sides together (RST), with ¼" of B extending beyond as shown. Holding one piece in each hand, bring curved edges together as they feed under the presser foot while stitching a ¼" seam (see page 12). Repeat to sew all AB sets. Press seam towards A.

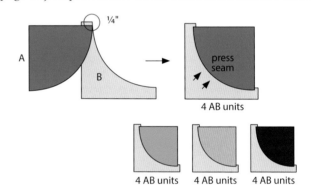

¼"
A
B
press seam
4 AB units

4 AB units   4 AB units   4 AB units

Square Up the Units

3. Square up the AB units to 4" x 4". Position WCR on blocks as shown with the blue dots on curved seams. Trim side and top. Rotate block and align trimmed edges with 4" marks and trim remaining fabric. Repeat for all AB units.

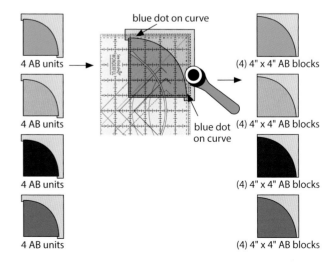

blue dot on curve

4 AB units
4 AB units
4 AB units
4 AB units

blue dot on curve

(4) 4" x 4" AB blocks
(4) 4" x 4" AB blocks
(4) 4" x 4" AB blocks
(4) 4" x 4" AB blocks

Assemble the Block

4. Lay out units as shown. Sew to form rows. Press seams open. Sew rows together. Press seams open.

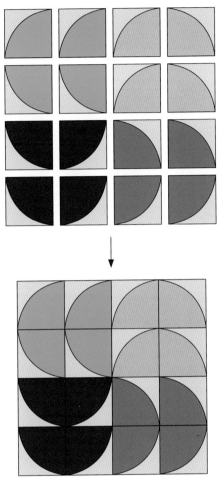

Block Assembly Diagram

Alternate Color & Layout Options

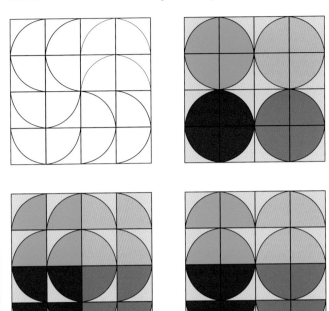

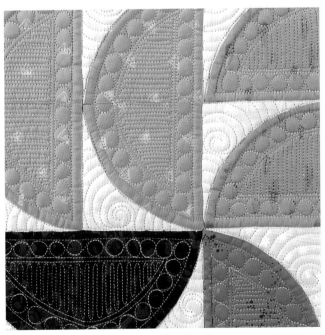

Custom Quilting Detail

Block 28 - Fan Dance

Unfinished block size: 14½" x 14½"

MATERIALS FOR 1 BLOCK
✛ 1 each 8" x 20" focus fabric in coral and orange
✛ (1) 5" x 5" accent fabric in blue
✛ 1 fat quarter neutral background fabric
✛ Wonder Curve Ruler™ (WCR)

GENERAL CUTTING:

From each coral and orange focus fabric, cut:
✛ (4) 5½" x 5½" squares
✛ (1) 2¾" x 4½" rectangle

From blue accent fabric, cut:
✛ (1) 4¼" x 4¼" square

From background fabric, cut:
✛ (1) 5¾" x 5¾" square
✛ (2) 5" x 5" squares
✛ (6) 4" x 4" squares

Cut the Curves

Refer to pages 13 and 14 to cut the following Twist, Shimmer, and Antler curves with the WCR.

Orange focus fabric:
Twist C
From the 2¾" x 4½" rectangle, cut one C curve right side down (RSD).

1 C cut
RSD

Coral focus fabric:
Twist C
From the 2¾" x 4½" rectangle, cut one C curve right side up (RSU).

1 C cut
RSU

Blue accent fabric:
Shimmer A
From the 4¼" x 4¼" square, cut one A curve.

1 A

Background fabric:
Shimmer B
From the 5¾" x 5¾" square cut in half diagonally, cut two B curves.

2 B

Antler F
From two 5" x 5" squares, cut one F curve RSU and one F curve RSD.

1 F cut RSU   1 F cut RSD

Sew Half-Square Triangle Units

1. Make eight half-square triangle (HST) units. Draw diagonal line on wrong side of four 5½" orange squares. Layer, RST, with four 5½" coral squares. Sew a ¼" seam on each side of drawn line. Cut on drawn line. Press open.

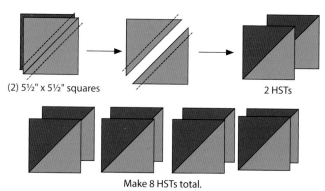

(2) 5½" x 5½" squares   2 HSTs

Make 8 HSTs total.

2. Cut three HST units with the WCR to make HST A and HST B curves. Position WCR on HST as shown. Ensure colors are oriented as shown. Discard pieces not used.

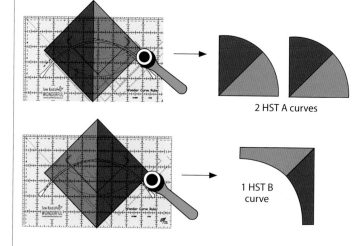

2 HST A curves

1 HST B curve

Sew the Curves
3. Lay out the following sets:

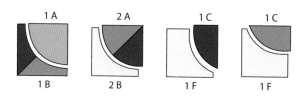

1 A   2 A   1 C   1 C

1 B   2 B   1 F   1 F

4. Position A on B, right sides together (RST), with ¼" of B extending beyond A as shown. Holding one piece in each hand, bring curved edges together as they feed under the presser foot while stitching a ¼" seam (see page 12). Repeat to sew all AB sets. Press seam towards A.

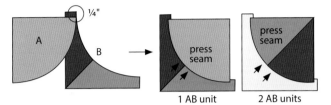

5. Position C on F, RST, as shown matching ends and leaving a ¾" tail as indicated. Sew curved seam. Press seam towards F.

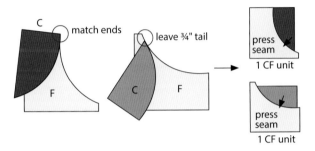

Square Up the Units

6. Square up AB units to 4" x 4". Position WCR on blocks as shown with the blue dots on curved seams. Trim side and top. Rotate block and align trimmed edges with 4" marks and trim remaining fabric. Repeat for all AB units.

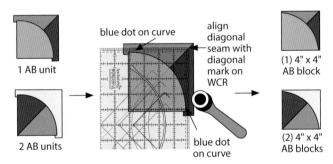

7. Square up the five remaining HST units to 4" x 4".

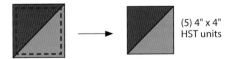

8. Square up the CF unit to 4" x 4". Position WCR on blocks as shown with the blue dot and 2" mark on curved seams. Trim side and top. Rotate block and align trimmed edges with 4" marks and trim remaining fabric. Repeat for all CF units.

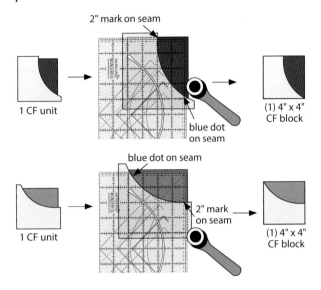

Assemble the Block

9. Lay out units as shown. Sew to form rows. Press seams open. Sew rows together, then press seams open.

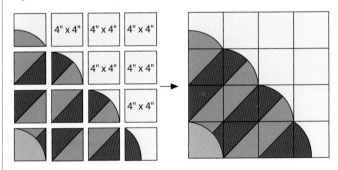

Alternate Color & Layout Options

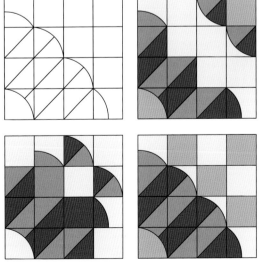

Block Assembly Diagram

Block 29 - Dancing Queen

Unfinished block size: 14½" x 14½"

MATERIALS FOR 1 BLOCK
✢ 1 each fat quarter focus fabric in fuchsia and pink
✢ 1 fat quarter neutral background fabric
✢ Wonder Curve Ruler™ (WCR)

GENERAL CUTTING
From each fuchsia and pink focus fabric, cut:
✢ (8) 5" x 5" squares
From background fabric, cut:
✢ (8) 5¾" x 5¾" squares

Cut the curves

Refer to pages 13 and 14 to cut the following Antler and Shimmer curves with the WCR.

Fuchsia focus fabric:
Antler F

From eight 5" x 5" squares, cut four F curves and four C curves right side up (RSU) and four F and four C curves right side down (RSD).

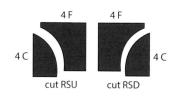

4 F   4 F
4 C   4 C
cut RSU   cut RSD

Pink focus fabric:
Antler F

From eight 5" x 5" squares, cut four F curves and four C curves RSU and four F and four C curves RSD.

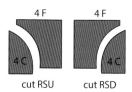

4 F   4 F
4 C   4 C
cut RSU   cut RSD

Background fabric:
Shimmer B

From eight 5¾" x 5¾" squares cut in half diagonally, cut sixteen B curves.

16 B

Sew the Curves

1. Lay out the following sets:

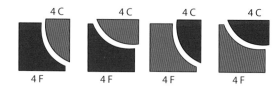

4 C   4 C   4 C   4 C
4 F   4 F   4 F   4 F

2. Position C on F, right sides together (RST), as shown, matching ends and leaving a ¾" tail as indicated. Sew curved seam (see page 12). Press seam towards F.

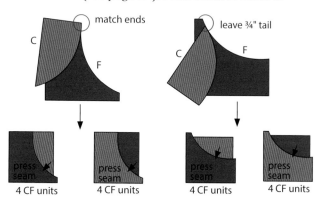

match ends   leave ¾" tail

press seam   press seam   press seam   press seam
4 CF units   4 CF units   4 CF units   4 CF units

3. Position WCR on CF units as shown with circle on V line on curved seam. Cut in the curve cut-out. Discard small piece cut off. Repeat for all CF units.

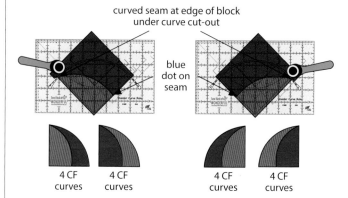

curved seam at edge of block under curve cut-out

blue dot on seam

4 CF curves   4 CF curves   4 CF curves   4 CF curves

4. Position CF on B pieces, RST, as shown, leaving a ¼" tail. Sew the curved seam to make CFB. Press seam towards B.

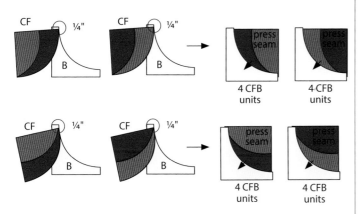

Square Up the Units

5. Square up CFB blocks to 4" x 4". Position WCR on blocks as shown with blue dots on curved seam and point. Trim side and top. Rotate block and align trimmed edges with 4" marks and trim remaining fabric. Repeat for all CFB units.

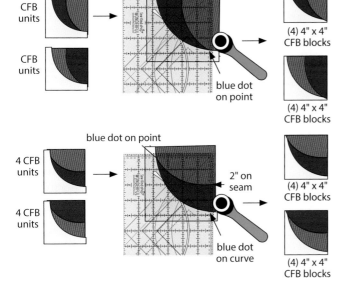

Assemble the Block

6. Lay out units as shown. Sew to form rows. Press seams open. Sew rows together. Press seams open.

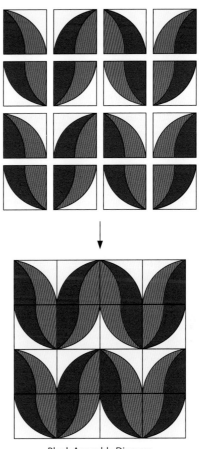

Block Assembly Diagram

Alternate Color & Layout Options

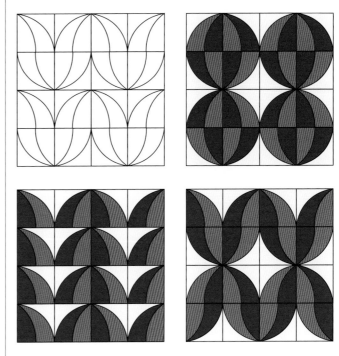

Block 30 - Oasis

Unfinished block size: 14½" x 14½"

MATERIALS FOR 1 BLOCK
✣ 1 each 10" x 10" focus fabric in sage and gold
✣ (1) 12" x 20" focus fabric in aqua
✣ (1) 10" x 20" neutral background fabric
✣ Wonder Curve Ruler™ (WCR)

GENERAL CUTTING
From sage focus fabric, cut:
✣ (4) 5" x 5" squares
From gold focus fabric, cut:
✣ (4) 4¼" x 4¼" squares
From aqua focus fabric, cut:
✣ (6) 5¾" x 5¾" squares
From background fabric, cut:
✣ (8) 5" x 5" squares

Cut the Curves

Refer to page 13 to cut the following Shimmer curves with the WCR.

Sage focus fabric:
Shimmer A and B
From four 5" x 5" squares, cut four A curves and four B curves.

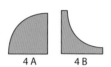

Aqua focus fabric:
Shimmer B
From six 5¾" x 5¾" squares cut in half diagonally, cut twelve B curves.

Gold focus fabric:
Shimmer A
From four 4¼" x 4¼" squares, cut four A curves.

Background fabric:
Shimmer A and B
From (8) 5" x 5" squares, cut eight A curves and eight B curves.

Sew the Curves

1. Lay out the following sets:

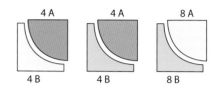

2. Position A on B, right sides together (RST), with ¼" of B extending beyond A as shown. Holding one piece in each hand, bring curved edges together as they feed under the presser foot while stitching a ¼" seam (see page 12). Repeat to sew all AB sets. Press seam towards A.

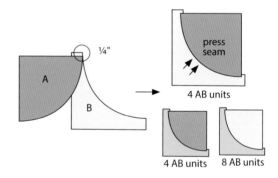

3. Working with green and background AB units and gold and aqua AB units, position AB under WCR with curved seam aligned with the blue curved line as shown. Cut in the curve cut-out. Discard small pieces.

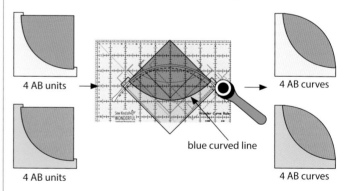

4. Lay out AB trimmed units and four background B pieces and four sage B units. Position AB on B, RST, with a ¼ " tail of B extending beyond AB as shown. Sew curved seam to make ABB units. Press seam towards B. Repeat for remaining set.

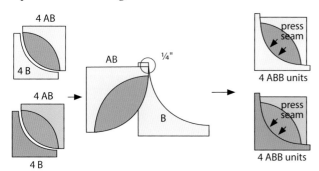

Square Up the Units

5. Square up the AB units and ABB units to 4" x 4". Position WCR on blocks as shown with the blue dots on curved seams or points. Trim side and top. Rotate block and align trimmed edges with 4" marks and trim remaining fabric. Repeat for all AB and ABB units.

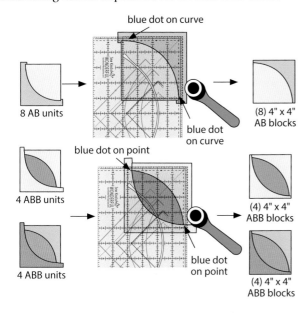

Assemble the Units

6. Lay out units as shown. Sew to form rows. Press seams open. Sew rows together, then press seams open.

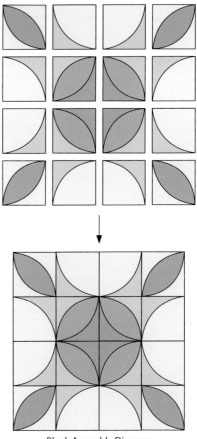

Block Assembly Diagram

Alternate Color & Layout Options

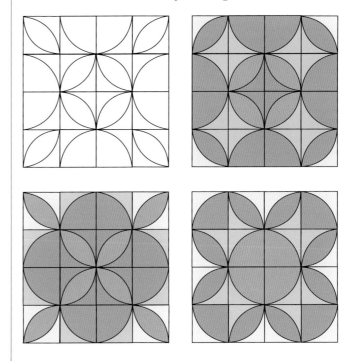

Quilt Patterns

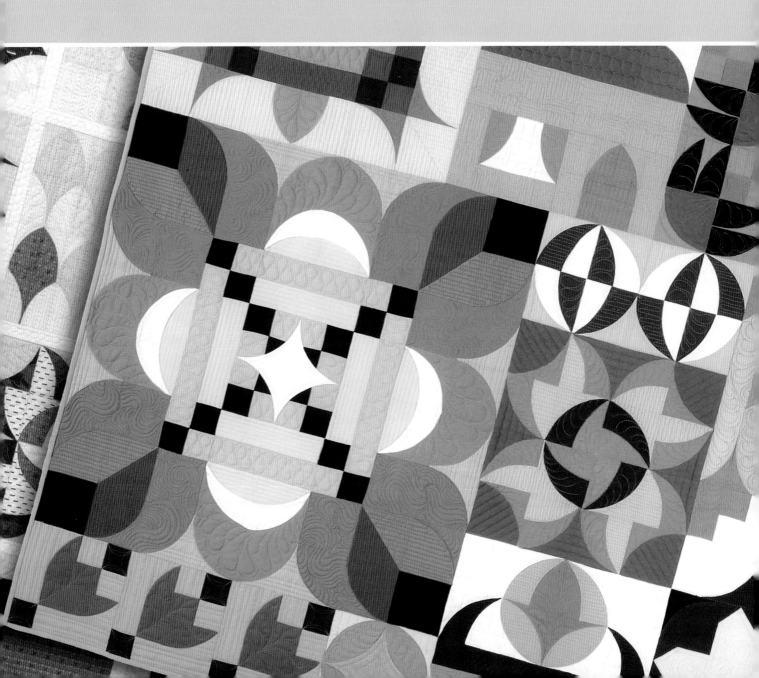

Dream Bigger Sampler Quilt

Finished size: 70" x 84"

We love a good sampler quilt! This quilt will definitely remain on our "Top 10 Favorite Quilts" list. Creating all these awesome blocks was so fun and seeing them all come together in one quilt is quite satisfying—eye candy at its finest!

MATERIALS

(*Note:* These are very generous fabric amounts. We recommend working from the materials box for each block.)

+ 36 fat quarters in assorted colors
+ 12 background ½ yard cuts in assorted colors
+ 6¾ yards backing fabric
+ ¾ yard binding fabric
+ Wonder Curve Ruler™ (WCR)

Instructions

1. Make one of each of the 30 blocks in this book. Lay out each block as in the Block Assembly Diagram or create your own layout.

2. Sew blocks together to form rows. Press seams open.

3. Sew rows together. Press seams open.

4. Quilt and bind as desired.

TIP: Dream Bigger and Mod Sampler are great examples of how the same 30 blocks can feel completely different. Dream Bigger focused on each block holding its own in color and design next to all its neighbors, whereas Mod Sampler played with colors purposefully blending into the neighboring blocks and creating a softer feel with 1" (2.5cm) sashing between blocks. Both layouts are very appealing and make two beautiful quilts.

Mod Sampler Quilt

Finished size: 76" x 91"

We love making monochromatic quilts and blocks! They always feel very organized. We really wanted this sampler quilt to feel as if the color was slowly moving around the quilt. It is still full spectrum but very organized, which makes us very happy!

MATERIALS

(*Note:* These are very generous fabric amounts. We recommend working from the materials box for each block.)

+ 36 fat quarters in assorted colors
+ 12 background ½ yard cuts in assorted colors
+ 1½ yards sashing and border fabric
+ 7½ yards backing fabric
+ ¾ yard binding fabric
+ Wonder Curve Ruler™ (WCR)

GENERAL CUTTING

Follow cutting instructions on individual blocks.

From sashing fabric, cut:
+ (1) 14½" x width of fabric (WOF); from strip, cut (24) 1½" x 14½" strips for sashing between blocks
+ (19) 1½" x WOF; sew strips together end to end, then cut (5) 1½" x 74½" strips for sashing between rows (2) 1½" x 89½" strips for side borders (2) 1½" x 76½" strips for top and bottom borders

Instructions

1. Make one of each of the 30 blocks in this book. Choose desired layout or follow the Block Assembly Diagram for each block.

2. Sew a 1½" x 14½" sashing strip between blocks on each row. Press seams.

3. Sew a 1½" x 74½" sashing strip between each row. Press seams.

4. Sew a 1½" x 89½" border strip to each side of quilt center. Press seams.

5. Sew a 1½" x 76½" border strip to top and bottom of quilt. Press seams.

6. Quilt and bind as desired.

Thirty Something Sampler Quilt

Finished size: 70" x 84"

We love to work with asymmetrical designs. We like things to be just a tad different. Here we took all 30 blocks—combined some, deconstructed others, and then balanced things out with color and the remaining individual blocks. We love the color play across the quilt and the different sizes of blocks. We really love the willow tree block that was created by combining the Beech Tree and Shell Chain blocks.

MATERIALS
(*Note:* These are very generous fabric amounts. We recommend working from the materials box for each block.)
+ (12) ½ yard cuts in assorted colors
+ 18 fat quarters in assorted colors
+ 12 background ½ yard cuts in assorted colors
+ 6¾ yards backing fabric
+ ¾ yard binding fabric
+ Wonder Curve Ruler™ (WCR)

Instructions

1. Read through the specific block instructions for each section.

2. Cut fabric in the order listed for each fabric color.

3. Press curved seams to the side and straight seams open. This helps manage the bulk in intersections when units are sewn into blocks.

4. Assemble blocks in sections as indicated on each Block Assembly Diagram. Then sew sections together.

5. Sew sampler blocks together into sections as shown on Quilt Assembly Diagram (page 92). Press seams. Sew sections together. Press seams.

6. Quilt and bind as desired.

Sampler Blocks

Make one each of the following blocks:
+ Block 2 - Petal Pusher, page 20
+ Block 8 - Birdie, page 32
+ Block 10 - Sunburst, page 36
+ Block 11 - Basket, page 40
+ Block 13 - Reflection, page 46
+ Block 14 - Whirligig, page 48
+ Block 16 - Bungalow, page 52
+ Block 19 - Flower Show, page 58
+ Block 21 - Stair Stepper, page 62

MODIFIED SAMPLER BLOCKS

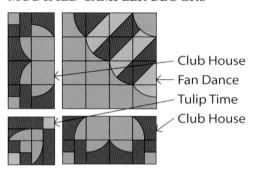

Club House
Fan Dance
Tulip Time
Club House

Unfinished block size: 21½" x 21½"

BLOCKS USED
+ Block 28 - Fan Dance, page 76
+ Block 12 - Club House, page 44
+ Block 25 - Tulip Time, page 70 (¼ of block)

MATERIALS:
+ ½ yard sage focus fabric
+ (1) 12" x 20" gold focus fabric
+ ½ yard maroon background fabric

GENERAL CUTTING
From sage, cut:
+ (1) 5¾" x 5¾" square for B curves
+ (2) 5" x 5" squares for F and C curves
+ (1) 4¼" x 4¼" square for A curves
+ (10) 4" x 4" squares
+ (6) 2¼" x 2¼" squares for 4-patch and 3-patch units
+ (8) 2¾" x 4½" rectangles for C curves

From gold, cut:
+ (4) 5½" x 5½" squares for half-square triangle (HST) units
+ (1) 2¾" x 4½" rectangle for C curves
+ (2) 2¼" x 2¼" squares for 4-patch units

From maroon, cut:
+ (4) 5½" x 5½" squares for HST units
+ (8) 5" x 5" squares for F curves
+ (1) 2¾" x 4½" rectangle for C curves
+ (2) 3½" x 5" rectangles for D curves
+ (6) 2¼" x 2¼" squares for 4-patch and 3-patch units
+ (4) 2¼" x 4" rectangles for 3-patch units
+ (2) 2¼" x 5¾" rectangles for sashing

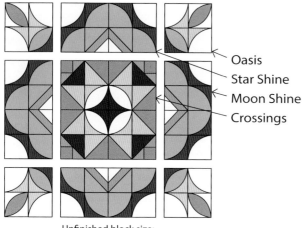

Oasis
Star Shine
Moon Shine
Crossings

Unfinished block size:
28½" x 28½"

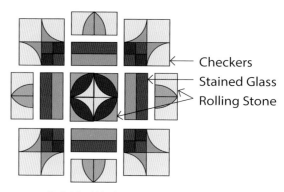

Checkers
Stained Glass
Rolling Stone

Unfinished block size:
21½" x 21½"

BLOCKS USED

+ Block 18 - Star Shine, page 56
+ Block 24 - Crossings, page 68
+ Block 26 - Moon Shine, page 72
+ Block 30 - Oasis, page 80

MATERIALS

+ 1 fat quarter in gray
+ ⅓ yard focus fabric in yellow
+ ½ yard focus fabric in peach
+ ⅓ yard focus fabric in maroon
+ (1) 10" x 20" focus fabric in sage
+ ½ yard background fabric in white
+ (1) 10" x 20" focus fabric in burgundy

GENERAL CUTTING

From gray focus fabric, cut:
+ (4) 5" x 5" squares for HST units
+ (4) 4¼" x 4¼" squares for A curves
+ (4) 2¼" x 2¼" squares for 3-patch/HST units
From yellow focus fabric, cut:
+ (8) 5¾" x 5¾" squares for B curves
+ (4) 5" x 5" squares for HST units
From peach focus fabric, cut:
+ (4) 5" x 5" squares for HST units
+ (20) 4¼" x 4¼" squares for A curves
From maroon focus fabric, cut:
+ (14) 5¾" x 5¾" squares for B curves
From sage focus fabric, cut:
+ (4) 5" x 5" squares for HST units
+ (8) 2¼" x 2¼" squares for 3-patch/HST units
From white focus fabric, cut:
+ (4) 5¾" x 5¾" squares for B curves
+ (20) 4¼" x 4¼" squares for A curves
+ (8) 2¼" x 2¼" squares for snowball corner units
From burgundy focus fabric, cut:
+ (2) 5¾" x 5¾" squares for B curves
+ (4) 4" x 4" squares for 3-patch/HST units

BLOCKS USED

+ Block 4 - Stained Glass, page 24
+ Block 17 - Rolling Stone, page 54
+ Block 22 - Checkers, page 64

MATERIALS

+ (1) 12" x 12" focus fabric in gray
+ (1) 12" x 20" focus fabric in sage
+ (1) 8" x 20" focus fabric in wine
+ (1) 8" x 20" focus fabric in maroon
+ (1) 5" x 20" focus fabric in peach
+ ½ yard light pink background fabric

GENERAL CUTTING

From gray focus fabric, cut:
+ (4) 5¾" x 5¾" squares for B curves
From sage focus fabric, cut:
+ (2) 5¾" x 5¾" squares for B curves
+ (8) 2¾" x 4½" rectangles for C curves
From wine focus fabric, cut:
+ (4) 4¼" x 4¼" squares for A curves
+ (8) 2¼" x 2¼" squares for 4-patch units
From maroon focus fabric, cut:
+ (4) 2¼" x 7½" rectangles for sashing
+ (8) 2¼" x 2¼" squares for 4-patch units
From peach focus fabric, cut:
+ (4) 2¼" x 7½" rectangles for sashing
From light pink background fabric, cut:
+ (2) 5¾" x 5¾" squares for B curves
+ (8) 5" x 5" squares for F curves
+ (8) 4¼" x 4¼" squares for A curves
+ (4) 4" x 4" squares

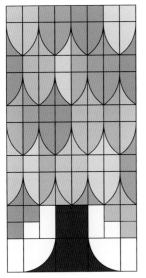

Note: This is a design wall block. Cut curved pieces and lay out all tree block pieces before sewing curves. Sew curved sets one at a time and place back on layout. Square up one block at a time and place back on layout. Sew to form rows. Press seams open. Sew rows together, then press seams open.

Unfinished block size:
14½" x 28½"

BLOCKS USED
✢ Block 1 - Shell Chain, page 18
✢ Block 7 - Beech Tree, page 30

MATERIALS
✢ (5) 10" x 20" assorted tree fabrics light tan, sage, gold, light green, and light gold
✢ (1) 5" x 20" accent fabric in pink
✢ (1) 6" x 20" tree trunk fabric in wine
✢ (1) 5" x 20" background fabric in white

GENERAL CUTTING
From the light tan tree fabric, cut:
✢ (4) 3½" x 5" rectangles for C and D curves
✢ (2) 2¾" x 4½" rectangles for C curves
✢ (6) 2¼" x 2¼" squares
From the sage tree fabric, cut:
✢ (6) 3½" x 5" rectangles for C and D curves
✢ (6) 2¼" x 2¼" squares
From the gold tree fabric, cut:
✢ (6) 3½" x 5" rectangles for C and D curves
✢ (9) 2¼" x 2¼" squares
From the light green tree fabric, cut:
✢ (4) 3½" x 5" rectangles for C and D curves
✢ (2) 2¾" x 4½" rectangles for C curves
✢ (6) 2¼" x 2¼" squares
From the light gold tree fabric, cut:
✢ (8) 3½" x 5" rectangles for C and D curves
✢ (7) 2¼" x 2¼" rectangles
From pink accent fabric, cut:
✢ (4) 3½" x 5" rectangles for C and D curves
✢ (4) 2¼" x 2¼" squares
From wine tree trunk fabric, cut:
✢ (1) 5¾" x 5¾" square for B curves
✢ (2) 4" x 4" squares
From white background fabric, cut:
✢ (2) 4¼" x 4¼" squares for A curves
✢ (4) 2¼" x 4" rectangles
✢ (2) 2¼" x 2¼" squares

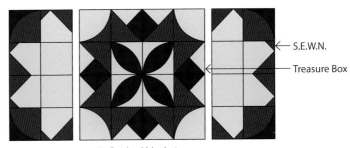

←— S.E.W.N.

←— Treasure Box

Unfinished block size:
14½" x 28½"

BLOCKS USED
✢ Block 5 - Treasure Box, page 26
✢ Block 15 - S.E.W.N., page 50

MATERIALS:
✢ ½ yard focus fabric in light blue
✢ 1 fat quarter focus fabric in black
✢ ½ yard focus fabric in red

GENERAL CUTTING
From light blue focus fabric, cut:
✢ (4) 5¾" x 5¾" squares for B curves
✢ (2) 5½" x 5½" squares for half-quarter triangle (HQT) units
✢ (4) 4¼" x 4¼" squares for A curves
✢ (12) 4" x 4" squares
From black focus fabric, cut:
✢ (2) 5¾" x 5¾" squares for B curves
✢ (2) 5½" x 5½" squares for HQT units
✢ (4) 4¼" x 4¼" squares for A curves
From red focus fabric, cut:
✢ (2) 5¾" x 5¾" squares for B curves
✢ (4) 5" x 5" squares for HQT units
✢ (4) 4¼" x 4¼" squares for A curves
✢ (8) 2¾" x 2¾" squares for snowball corner units
✢ (8) 1¾" x 1¾" squares for snowball corner units

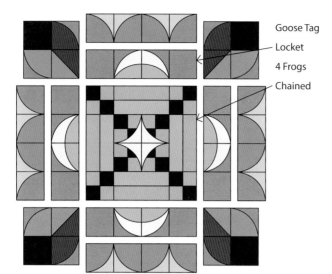

Goose Tag
Locket
4 Frogs
Chained

Unfinished block size:
28½" x 28½"

BLOCKS USED

+ Block 3 - Goose Tag, page 22
+ Block 9 - Locket, page 34
+ Block 20 - 4 Frogs, page 60
+ Block 23 - Chained, page 66

MATERIALS:

+ (1) 10" x 20" focus fabric in black
+ (1) 5" x 20" focus fabric in maroon
+ (1) 5" x 20" focus fabric in light purple
+ ½ yard focus fabrc in gray
+ 1 fat quarter focus fabric in gold
+ 1 fat quarter focus fabric in light green
+ 1 fat quarter focus fabric in white
+ (1) 10" x 20" focus fabric in blue
+ (1) fat quarter focus fabric in peach

GENERAL CUTTING

From black focus fabric, cut:
+ (4) 4" x 4" squares
+ (4) 2½" x 2½" squares for 4-patch units
+ (12) 2¼" x 2¼" squares for 4-patch units

From each maroon and light purple focus fabrics, cut:
+ (2) 5" x 5" squares for HST units
+ (2) 4¼" x 4¼" squares for A curves

From gray focus fabric, cut:
+ (4) 5¾" x 5¾" squares for B curves
+ (8) 4¼" x 4¼" squares for A curves
+ (8) 4" x 4" squares

From gold focus fabric, cut:
+ (8) 5" x 5" squares for A and B curves

From light green focus fabric, cut:
+ (8) 5¾" x 5¾" squares for B curves

From white focus fabric, cut:
+ (2) 5¾" x 5¾" squares for B curves
+ (8) 5" x 5" squares for F curves

From blue focus fabric, cut:
+ (4) 2¼" x 7½" rectangles for sashing
+ (8) 2¾" x 4½" rectangles for C curves

From peach focus fabric, cut:
+ (4) 2¼" x 7½" rectangles for sashing
+ (8) 2¼" x 2¼" squares for 4-patch units
+ (8) 2¼" x 2½" squares for 4-patch units

BLOCKS USED

+ Block 27 - Bridges, page 74

MATERIALS

+ (1) 10" x 20" focus fabric in orange
+ (1) 12" x 12" focus fabric in sage

GENERAL CUTTING

From orange focus fabric (color 1), cut:
+ (8) 4¼" x 4¼" squares for A curves

From sage focus fabric (color 2), cut:
+ (4) 5¾" x 5¾" squares for B curves

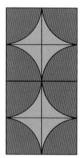

Unfinished
block size:
7½" x 14½"

BLOCKS USED

+ Block 27 - Bridges, page 74

MATERIALS

+ (1) 10" x 20" focus fabric in orange
+ (1) 12" x 12" focus fabric in sage

GENERAL CUTTING

From orange focus fabric, cut:
+ (8) 4¼" x 4¼" squares for A curves

From sage focus fabric, cut:
+ (4) 5¾" x 5¾" squares for B curves

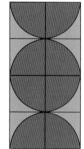

Unfinished
block size:
7½" x 14½"

BLOCKS USED
+ Block 4 - Stained Glass, page 24
+ Block 29 - Dancing Queen, page 78

MATERIALS
+ (1) 5" x 20" focus fabric in pink
+ (1) 5" x 20" focus fabric in light pink
+ (1) 6" x 12" focus fabric in gray
+ (1) 5" x 15" focus fabric in red
+ (1) 4" x 4" focus fabric in white

GENERAL CUTTING
From each pink and light pink focus fabric, cut:
+ (2) 5" x 5" squares for F curves
+ (2) 2¾" x 4½" rectangles for C curves
From gray focus fabric, cut:
+ (2) 5¾" x 5¾" squares for B curves
From red focus fabric, cut:
+ (2) 2¼" x 7½" rectangles for sashing
+ (2) 2¼" x 4" rectangles for sashing
From white focus fabric, cut:
+ (1) 4" x 4" square

Unfinished block size: 7½" x 14½"

BLOCKS USED
+ Block 9 - Locket, page 34
+ Block 29 - Dancing Queen, page 78

MATERIALS
+ 1 each 5" x 20" focus fabric in light pink and maroon
+ (1) 6" x 12" focus fabric in yellow
+ (1) 10" x 10" focus fabric in green
+ (1) 12" x 12" background fabric in light yellow

Unfinished block size: 7½" x 14½"

GENERAL CUTTING
From each light pink and maroon focus fabric, cut:
+ (2) 5" x 5" squares for F curves
+ (2) 2¾" x 4½" rectangles for C curves
From yellow focus fabric, cut:
+ (2) 5¾" x 5¾" squares for B curves
From green focus fabric, cut:
+ (4) 5" x 5" squares for F curves
From light yellow background fabric, cut:
+ (2) 5¾" x 5¾" squares for B curves
+ (4) 2¾" x 4½" rectangles

BLOCK USED
+ Block 29 - Dancing Queen, page 78

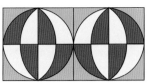

Unfinished block size: 7½" x 14½"

MATERIALS
+ 1 each 10" x 20" focus fabric in orange and white
+ (1) 12" x 12" background fabric in mustard

GENERAL CUTTING
From each orange and white focus fabric, cut:
+ (4) 5" x 5" squares for F curves
+ (4) 2¾" x 4½" rectangles for C curves
From mustard background fabric, cut:
+ (4) 5¾" x 5¾" squares for B curves

BLOCK USED
+ Block 4 - Stained Glass, page 24

Unfinished block size: 7½" x 7½"

MATERIALS:
+ (1) 10" x 10" focus fabric in peach
+ 1 each 6" x 12" focus fabric in gray and blue

GENERAL CUTTING
From peach focus fabric, cut:
+ (4) 4¼" x 4¼" squares for A curves
From each gray and blue focus fabric, cut:
+ (2) 5¾" x 5¾" squares for B curves

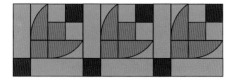

Unfinished block size:
7½" x 21½"

BLOCK USED
✛ Block 25 - Tulip Time, page 70

MATERIALS
✛ (1) 10" x 20" focus fabric in orange
✛ (1) 6" x 10" accent fabric in wine
✛ 1 fat quarter background fabric in gold

GENERAL CUTTING
From orange focus fabric, cut:
✛ (6) 2¾" x 4½" rectangles for C curves
✛ (6) 2¼" x 2¼" squares for 4-patch units
From wine accent fabric, cut:
✛ (6) 2¼" x 2¼" squares for 4-patch units
From gold focus fabric, cut:
✛ (6) 3½" x 5" rectangles for D curves
✛ (6) 2¼" x 5¾" rectangles for sashing
✛ (6) 2¼" x 2¼" squares for 4-patch units

BLOCK USED
✛ Block 6 - Lotus Blossom, page 28

MATERIALS
✛ (1) 8" x 20" focus fabric in light gray
✛ (1) 12" x 20" focus fabric in black
✛ ½ yard focus fabric in gold

GENERAL CUTTING
From light gray focus fabric, cut:
✛ (4) 4¼" x 4¼" squares for A curves
✛ (8) 2¼" x 2¼" squares for 4-patch units
From black focus fabric, cut:
✛ (16) 2¾" x 4½" rectangles for C curves
From gold focus fabric, cut:
✛ (2) 5¾" x 5¾" squares for B curves
✛ (16) 3½" x 5" rectangles for D curves
✛ (8) 2¼" x 2¼" squares for 4-patch units

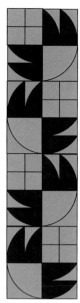

Unfinished
block size:
7½" x 28½"

Quilt Assembly Diagram

Assembly Instructions

1. Sew blocks together into sections as shown. Press seams open.

2. Sew sections together. Press seams open.

3. Quilt and bind as desired.

Favorite Things Quilt

Finished size: 28" x 70"

We love these five blocks together in this runner! It's perfect on a bed, as a table runner, or as a wall hanging.

MATERIALS

+ 10 fat quarters in assorted colors
+ 10 fat eighths in assorted colors
+ 2½ yards background fabric
+ 2½ yards backing fabric
+ ½ yard binding fabric
+ Wonder Curve Ruler™ (WCR)

Instructions

1. Make two each of the following blocks:
- Block 7 - Beech Tree, page 30
- Block 8 - Birdie, page 32
- Block 11 - Basket, page 40
- Block 16 - Bungalow, page 52
- Block 19 - Flower Show, page 58

2. Lay out blocks as shown. Sew to form rows. Press seams open.

3. Sew rows together. Press seams open.

4. Quilt and bind as desired.

TIP: Lay out blocks with multiple arrangements to choose the most appealing for color and fabric choices.

S.E.W.N. Quilt

Finished size: 42" x 42"

This quilt's name has a double meaning. Can you figure it out? There are beautiful quilting spaces in this quilt to show off your fancy hand or machine quilting.

MATERIALS

- ✛ (2) ¾ yard cuts of assorted focus fabrics in yellow and mustard
- ✛ 2 yards white background fabric
- ✛ 1½ yards backing fabric
- ✛ ½ yard binding fabric
- ✛ Wonder Curve Ruler™ (WCR)

Instructions

1. Make nine S.E.W.N. blocks (page 50). Sew five blocks with the mustard focus fabric and four with the yellow focus fabric.

2. Lay out blocks as shown. Sew to form rows. Press seams open.

3. Sew rows together. Press seams open.

4. Quilt and bind as desired.

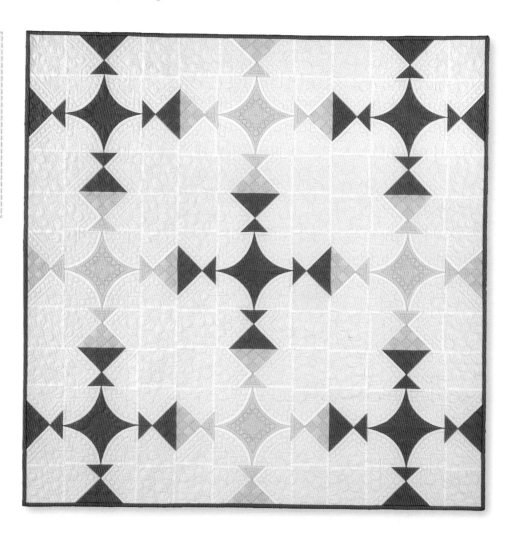

> **TIP:** This block has multiple alternative layouts, which create different secondary designs.

Whirligig Reflections Quilt

Finished size: 56" x 56"

We love the movement this quilt has with the combination of these two blocks! Sampler quilts have endless quilt variations by combining two, three, four, or more blocks.

MATERIALS
+ (8) ⅓ yard cuts assorted focus fabrics in light yellow
+ ⅓ yard cuts focus fabrics in assorted dark yellows
+ 6 fat quarter focus fabrics in assorted greens
+ 3 yards white background fabric
+ 4 yards backing fabric
+ ½ yard binding fabric
+ Wonder Curve Ruler™ (WCR)

GENERAL CUTTING
From each ⅓ yard light yellow fabric, cut:
+ (1) 5¾" x width of fabric (WOF) strip; from strip, cut:
  • (4) 5¾" x 5¾" squares; then, cut in half diagonally
  • (12) 2¾" x 4½"
From each dark yellow ⅓ yard, cut:
+ (2) 5" x WOF; from strip, cut (12) 5" x 5" squares
From each green fat quarter, cut:
+ (8) 5" x 5" squares
  (*Note:* Use optional A and B cutting instructions on page 13)
From background fabric, cut:
+ (6) 5" x WOF strips; from strips, cut (48) 5" x 5" squares
  (*Note:* Use optional A and B cutting instructions on page 13)
+ (4) 4" x WOF strips; from strips, cut (32) 4" x 4" squares
+ (5) 5¾" x WOF strips; from strips, cut (32) 5¾" x 5¾" squares; then, cut in half diagonally
+ (4) 4¼" x WOF strips; from strips, cut (32) 4¼" x 4¼" squares

Instructions

1. Make eight blocks each, mixing light and dark colors in every block:
  • Block 13 - Reflection, page 46
  • Block 14 - Whirligig, page 48

2. Lay out blocks as shown. Sew to form rows. Press seams open.

3. Sew rows together. Press seams open.

4. Quilt and bind as desired.

TIP: Use solid background fabric to make blocks made with scrappy textured focus fabrics pop!

Moon Shine Path Quilt

Finished size: 70" x 70"

The Moon Shine block has a twin sister block. Can you figure out which one?

MATERIALS
- 17 fat quarters in assorted dark green focus fabrics
- ⅔ yard lime green focus fabric
- 2¼ yards citrine focus fabric
- 3¼ yards white background fabric
- 4½ yards backing fabric
- ⅔ yard binding fabric
- Wonder Curve Ruler™ (WCR)

GENERAL CUTTING
From each dark green fat quarter, cut:
- (6) 5¾" x 5¾" squares; then, cut each in half diagonally (102 total)
- (6) 2¾" x 2¾" squares (102 total; keep 96)
- (4) 2¼" x 2¼" squares (68 total; keep 52)
- (6) 1¾" x 1¾" squares (102 total; keep 96)

From each lime green and citrine fabric, cut:
- (4) 5" x width of fabric (WOF) strips; from strips, cut (26) 5" x 5" squares

From citrine fabric, cut:
- (12) 4¼" x WOF strips; from strips, cut (100) 4¼" x 4¼" squares

From background fabric, cut:
- (12) 4¼" x WOF strips; from strips, cut (104) 4¼" x 4¼" squares
- (15) 4" x WOF strips; from strips, cut (144) 4" x 4" squares

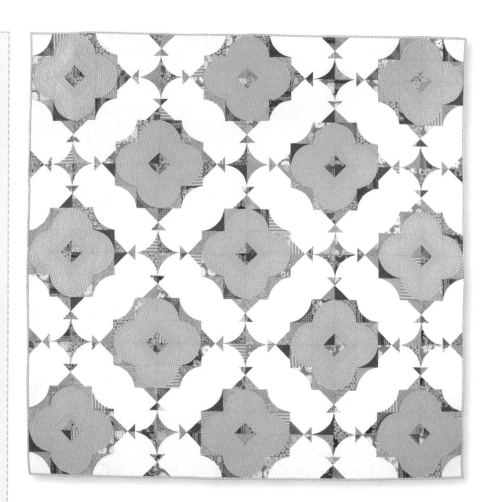

Instructions

1. Make twelve S.E.W.N. blocks (page 50) and thirteen Moon Shine blocks (page 72).

2. Lay out blocks as shown. Sew to form rows. Press seams open.

3. Sew rows together. Press seams open.

4. Quilt and bind as desired.

> **TIP:** Use fabrics that read solid to show off custom quilting in large open areas

Workout Quilt

Finished size: 56" x 56"

Challenge on! We challenge you to make this quilt completely from your stash of amazing fabrics that you have loved for days/months/years and not wanted to cut up until you could find the most perfect scrappy pattern that would justify cutting up those beauties that you were saving as part of your retirement plan. You can do it!

MATERIALS
- ✦ (112) 5" x 5" focus fabrics in assorted colors
- ✦ 17 fat quarters of assorted neutral background fabrics
- ✦ 4 yards backing fabric
- ✦ ½ yard binding fabric
- ✦ Wonder Curve Ruler™ (WCR)

GENERAL CUTTING
From assorted focus fabrics, cut:
- ✦ (64) 4¼" x 4¼" squares
- ✦ (48) 5" x 5" squares

From each of 16 assorted background fabrics, cut:
- ✦ (4) 5¾" x 5¾" squares; then, cut in half diagonally
- ✦ (3) 5" x 5" squares
- ✦ (5) 4" x 4" squares

From 1 neutral background fabric, cut:
- ✦ (16) 4" x 4" squares

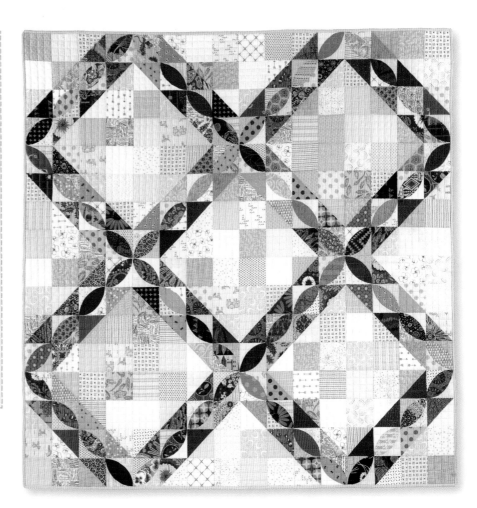

Instructions

1. Make sixteen Stair Stepper blocks (page 62).

2. Lay out as shown. Sew to form rows. Press seams open.

3. Sew rows together. Press seams open.

4. Quilt and bind as desired.

TIP: Be bold in choosing scrappy background fabrics which will add a lot of visual interest to the finished quilt. This quilt is a great example for choosing a wide variety of different values of neutral background fabrics.

Fan Dance Quilt

Finished size: 28" x 28"

We enjoyed playing with the layout and colors of this very fun modern version of the traditional fan block. We especially like how the stripes give it dimension and bring different sections to the foreground.

MATERIALS
+ 1 each ⅔ yard cuts focus fabrics in sienna and white
+ (1) ⅔ yard gray background fabric
+ 1 yard backing fabric
+ ½ yard binding fabric
+ Wonder Curve Ruler™ (WCR)

GENERAL CUTTING
From each sienna and white focus fabric, cut:
+ (3) 5½" x width of fabric (WOF) strip; from strips, cut (16) 5½" x 5½" squares
+ (1) 4½" x WOF strip; from strip, cut:
  • (4) 2¾" x 4½" rectangles
  • (4) 4" x 4" squares
From background fabric, cut:
+ (1) 5¾" x WOF strip; from strip, cut:
  • (4) 5¾" x 5¾" squares
  • (4) 4¼" x 4¼" squares
+ (1) 5" x WOF strips; from strips, cut (8) 5" x 5" squares
+ (2) 4" x WOF strips; from strips, cut (16) 4" x 4" squares

TIP: Use matchstick quilting to help a quilt lay flat that will be used as a wall hanging.

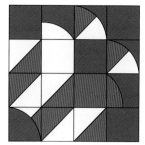

Fan Dance Block Variation

Instructions

1. Make four Fan Dance blocks (page 76) with variation shown.

2. Lay out blocks as shown. Sew to form rows. Press seams open.

3. Sew rows together. Press seams open.

4. Quilt and bind as desired.

Twisted Stones Quilt

Finished size: 28" x 70"

The Rolling Stone block looks so different in this layout that we bet you did a double take when you realized which sampler block was used to create this beauty! It's also great for using fabrics from your stash.

MATERIALS
+ 10 fat quarter focus fabrics in assorted greens, pinks, purples, and teals
+ 3 yards tan background fabric
+ 2¼ yards backing fabric
+ ½ yard binding fabric
+ Wonder Curve Ruler™ (WCR)

GENERAL CUTTING
From each fat quarter focus fabric, cut:
+ (4) 4¼" x 4¼" squares
+ (8) 2¾" x 4½" rectangles

From background fabric, cut:
+ (6) 5¾" x WOF strips; from strips cut (40) 5¾" x 5¾" squares
+ (10) 5" x WOF strips; from strips cut (80) 5" x 5" squares
+ (4) 4" x WOF strips; from strips cut:
  • (40) 4" x 4" squares

Instructions

1. Make ten Rolling Stone blocks (page 54).

2. Lay out blocks as shown. Sew to form rows. Press seams open.

3. Sew rows together. Press seams open.

4. Quilt and bind as desired.

Flying Birdies Quilt

Finished size: 42" x 49"

Everything about this quilt is fun, playful and happy—the perfect quilt to add a splash of color to any setting!

MATERIALS

✛ 25 assorted 6" x 20" fabrics for birdies
✛ 2½ yards white background fabric
✛ 3 yards backing fabric
✛ ½ yard binding fabric
✛ Wonder Curve Ruler™ (WCR)

GENERAL CUTTING

From each birdie fabric, cut:
✛ (3) 5¾" x 5¾" squares; then, cut each in half diagonally

From background fabric, cut:
✛ (17) 4¼" x width of fabric (WOF) strips; from strips, cut (150) 4¼" x 4¼" squares
✛ (2) 7½" x WOF strips; from strips, cut (7) 7½" x 7½" squares

Instructions

1. Make 150 basic Shimmer units (page 22). Sew to make birdie block with matching fabric.

2. Lay out in desired arrangement.
Note: There are five extra birdie units to use (or not) depending on your layout.

3. Working with one row at a time, sew two birdie units together as shown. Press seams open.

4. Sew row units together. Press seams open. Repeat for each row. Sew rows together. Press seams open.

5. Quilt and bind as desired.

> **TIP:** Use small scale prints to keep the focus on the pieced shapes.

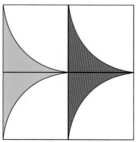

Shimmer block birdie unit
Make 35

Clubhouse Blues Quilt

Finished size: 70" x 84"

This quilt has an elegant and traditional look to it. I love the classic pink and blue combination and the secondary flower shape created when the blocks are sewn together.

MATERIALS
+ 4 yards focus fabric in blue
+ ¼ yard for 4-patch unit in pink
+ ¼ yard for 4-patch unit in black
+ 2¾ yards white background fabric
+ 5 yards backing fabric
+ ⅔ yard binding fabric
+ Wonder Curve Ruler™ (WCR)

GENERAL CUTTING
From blue focus fabric, cut:
+ (20) 5" x width of fabric (WOF) strips; from strips cut (160) 5" x 5" squares
+ (3) 7½" x WOF strips; from strips cut (40) 2¼" x 7½" rectangles
+ (3) 4" x WOF strips; from strips cut (40) 2¼" x 4" rectangles

From pink and black each 4-patch fabric, cut:
+ (3) 2¼" x WOF strips; from strips cut (40) 2¼" x 2¼" squares

From background fabric, cut:
+ (8) 4" x WOF strips; from strips cut (80) 4" x 4" squares
+ (12) 4½" x WOF strips; from strips cut (160) 2¾" x 4½" rectangles

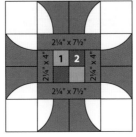

Clubhouse block

Instructions

1. Make 20 Clubhouse blocks (page 44) with center variation as shown.

2. Lay out blocks as shown. Sew to form rows. Press seams open.

3. Sew rows together. Press seams open.

4. Quilt and bind as desired.

Basket Chains Quilt

Finished size: 42" x 42"

We love the combination of these two blocks. They created this amazing quilt, which has multiple layers of design, dimension, and interest. The blocks merge to become part of each other.

MATERIALS

+ 14 assorted fat quarters for baskets, chains, and stars
+ (1) ½ yard neutral background fabric for Chained blocks
+ (5) 10" x 10" assorted fabrics for flowers
+ 2 yards white background fabric
+ 1½ yards backing fabric
+ ½ yard binding fabric
+ Wonder Curve Ruler™ (WCR)

Instructions

1. Make five Basket blocks (page 40) and four Chained blocks (page 66).

2. Lay out blocks as shown. Sew to form rows. Press seams open.

3. Sew rows together. Press seams open.

4. Quilt and bind as desired.

TIP: Use a neutral background fabric with a lot of texture to create a secondary design that gives a quilt an heirloom feel.

Froggy Tulips Quilt

Finished size: 42" x 42"

This quilt feels both modern with the large flower blocks and traditional with the chains working diagonally across the quilt. This is a great design to create from your stash and make really scrappy or try working with complimentary colors for lots of eye candy.

MATERIALS
+ 1 each ½ yard cuts focus fabrics in blue and black for large flowers and red for tulips
+ 1 each fat eighths focus fabric in blue, black, peach, dark peach, and black floral for chains
+ 2 yards neutral background fabric
+ Wonder Curve Ruler™ (WCR)

GENERAL CUTTING
Follow cutting instructions on block pages for focus fabrics.
From background fabric, cut:
+ (5) 5¾" x width of fabric (WOF) strips; from strips cut:
  • (16) 5¾" x 5¾" squares; then, cut in half diagonally
  • (20) 4" x 5¾" rectangles
+ (4) 5" x WOF strips; from strips cut (40) 3½" x 5" rectangles
+ (2) 4" x WOF strips; from strips cut (16) 4" x 4" squares
+ (3) 2¼" x WOF strips; from strips cut (40) 2¼" x 2¼" squares

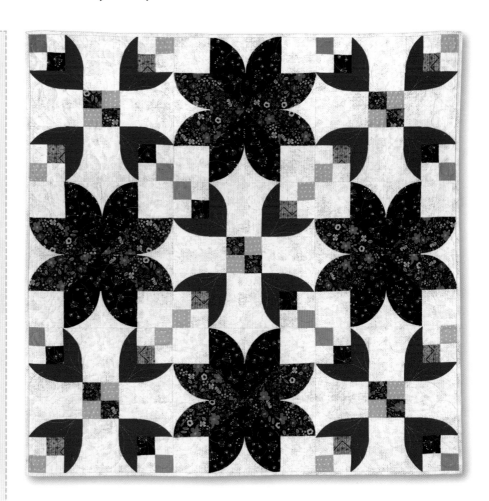

Instructions

1. Make five Tulip Time blocks with sashing variation as shown (page 70) and four 4 Frogs blocks (page 60).

2. Lay out blocks as shown. Sew to form rows. Press seams open.

3. Sew rows together. Press seams open.

4. Quilt and bind as desired.

TIP: Red and black colors have a lot of energy. Using them together creates balance throughout a quilt design.

COMMON METRIC CONVERSIONS

Measurements in this book do not include the metric equivalents. Refer to this chart to convert the most common measurements to metric.

¼" = 0.6cm	14½" = 36.8 cm
½" = 1.3cm	15" = 38 cm
¾" = 2cm	40" = 1.02m
1" = 2.5cm	41" = 1.04m
1¼" = 3.3cm	42" = 1.07m
1½" = 3.8cm	43" = 1.09m
1¾" = 4.4cm	44" = 1.12m
2" = 5cm	⅛ yard = 0.1m
2½" = 6.4cm	¼ yard = 0.2m
3" = 7.6cm	½ yard = 0.5m
3½" = 8.8cm	⅝ yard = 0.6m
4" = 10.2cm	¾ yard = 0.7m
4¼" = 10.8	1 yard = 0.9m
4½" = 11.4cm	1½ yards = 1.37m
5" = 12.7cm	2 yards = 1.8m
5½" = 14cm	2½ yards = 2.3m
5¾" = 14.6 cm	3 yard = 2.7m
6" = 15.2cm	3½ yards = 3.2m
6½" = 16.5cm	4 yards = 3.7m
7½" = 19.0 cm	4½ yards = 4.1m
10" = 25.4 cm	5 yards = 4.6m
12" = 30.5 cm	5½ yards = 5m
11" = 28.0 cm	

METRIC CONVERSION CHART

To Convert	To	Multiply By
inches	centimeters	2.54
centimeters	inches	0.4
feet	centimeters	30.5
centimeters	feet	0.03
yards	meters	0.9
meters	yards	1.1

Index